CW01390705

797,885 Books

are available to read at

Forgotten Books

www.ForgottenBooks.com

Forgotten Books' App
Available for mobile, tablet & eReader

Download on the
App Store

ANDROID APP ON
Google play

ISBN 978-1-332-62017-3
PIBN 10293852

This book is a reproduction of an important historical work. Forgotten Books uses state-of-the-art technology to digitally reconstruct the work, preserving the original format whilst repairing imperfections present in the aged copy. In rare cases, an imperfection in the original, such as a blemish or missing page, may be replicated in our edition. We do, however, repair the vast majority of imperfections successfully; any imperfections that remain are intentionally left to preserve the state of such historical works.

Forgotten Books is a registered trademark of FB &c Ltd.
Copyright © 2015 FB &c Ltd.
FB &c Ltd, Dalton House, 60 Windsor Avenue, London, SW19 2RR.
Company number 08720141. Registered in England and Wales.

For support please visit www.forgottenbooks.com

1 MONTH OF
FREE
READING

at

www.ForgottenBooks.com

By purchasing this book you are eligible for one month membership to ForgottenBooks.com, giving you unlimited access to our entire collection of over 700,000 titles via our web site and mobile apps.

To claim your free month visit: www.forgottenbooks.com/free293852

* Offer is valid for 45 days from date of purchase. Terms and conditions apply.

English
Français
Deutsche
Italiano
Español
Português

www.forgottenbooks.com

Mythology Photography **Fiction**
Fishing Christianity **Art** Cooking
Essays Buddhism Freemasonry
Medicine **Biology** Music **Ancient**
Egypt Evolution Carpentry Physics
Dance Geology **Mathematics** Fitness
Shakespeare **Folklore** Yoga Marketing
Confidence Immortality Biographies
Poetry **Psychology** Witchcraft
Electronics Chemistry History **Law**
Accounting **Philosophy** Anthropology
Alchemy Drama Quantum Mechanics
Atheism Sexual Health **Ancient History**
Entrepreneurship Languages Sport
Paleontology Needlework Islam
Metaphysics Investment Archaeology
Parenting Statistics Criminology
Motivational

(65)

EGYPTIAN RESEARCH ACCOUNT

NINTH YEAR

1903

THE OSIREION

AT ABYDOS

BY

MARGARET A. MURRAY

WITH SECTIONS BY

J. GRAFTON MILNE, B.A.

AND

W. E. CRUM, M.A.

200383
5/2/26

LONDON

BERNARD QUARITCH, 15, PICCADILLY, W.

1904

DT
57
B8
v.9

LONDON :
PRINTED BY GILBERT AND RIVINGTON, LTD.
ST. JOHN'S HOUSE, CLERKENWELL, E.C.

CONTENTS

LIST OF PLATES

WITH REFERENCES TO THE PAGES ON WHICH THEY ARE DESCRIBED

PREFACE

IN the winter of 1901-02 Mr. St. G. Caulfeild undertook the further examination of the temple of Sety at Abydos. Our work there resulted in finding the temenos wall, and showing the connection between the planning of that temple and the Royal Tombs of the early kings on the desert behind it. These results, and his careful study of the plan of the temple appeared in the last volume of the Research Account. But he also made other discoveries, which have been followed up during the next winter by Miss Murray, with the results here issued in this volume.

When Mr. Caulfeild began to excavate, I noticed some thick masses of crude brick, and suggested that they might be mastabas. He cleared along them and found that they formed a continuous wall, which we then identified as the temenos wall of the temple. I observed that parallel with this there was a slight long hollow on the surface, and proposed that he should clear it out. Some time after, on looking at the site, I was told the men had found desert a few feet down. This seemed strange, and on looking at it I saw that there was only blown sand. So they were told to go deeper. Again, after some time, on going there again, the same story of desert at the bottom was repeated; only this time about fifteen feet down. On examining it I found blown sand. So a third time they were told to go down, and soon after they struck some great blocks of limestone. The final result was that we found the pavement of the hall was forty-one feet under the surface; a depth filled up with some Roman rubbish and much blown sand over it.

After the excavations by Miss Murray and my wife, we realized that these great stones which we first found were the remains of the doorway to a limestone chamber near the north-west corner of the temenos, which had been entirely carried away for lime burning in Roman times. From the place of this doorway Mr. Caulfeild carried on excavations, continually expecting to come to an end of the entrance passage to the south, and find a door of approach to the subterranean constructions; but after continuing for a couple of hundred feet this seemed as far off as ever; and the season being at an end nothing more was done.

Miss Murray, then, entered on the work, with the certainty of a long inscribed passage to be cleared and copied, and its terminations to be found. Various attempts were made to settle the beginning of it by surface workings, tracing the filling of made earth which lay over it. And these resulted in showing that it turned at right angles, and led up towards the back doorway of the temple. But it could not be found at its beginning owing to the immense rubbish heaps thrown out in Mariette's clearing of the temple halls. The work was therefore concentrated on a point where the filling seemed to be undisturbed over the construction, hoping to find there the roof intact, and so enter an unbroken part of the passages. But on descending we found that the filling in had only been left because there was no roof under it there; and the whole of the ancient roofing had been removed, so far as we were able to ascertain, excepting one cracked lintel. Thus, nothing short of removing the whole forty feet of stuff over the whole construction can ever clear it. This season only sufficed for the trial working, and clearing the great hall, one chamber, and part of a passage. To do the whole clearance is beyond the slight resources of the Egyptian Research Account; and it is much to be hoped that the Department of Antiquities will undertake to open and maintain this unique hypogeum of Osiris as a part of the great temple which is one of the main attractions of Egypt.

It was most fortunate that we had the knowledge of Miss Murray and the artistic copying of Miss Hansard available for such a work, which required long and tedious facsimiles to be prepared, with due attention to the inscriptions. The elaborate study of Osiris which Miss Murray has here issued will, it is hoped, serve to clear up and emphasize the various aspects and connections of one of the fundamental deities of the Egyptian worship and beliefs.

W. M. F. P.

THE OSIREION

INTRODUCTION.

1. The excavations this year were carried on by Mrs. Petrie and myself. Mrs. Petrie managed the actual excavations, overseeing the men, paying the wages, in short, all the dull and uninteresting, though very necessary, part of the work, whereas I had the more congenial and amusing employment of copying the sculptures. Till the sculptures were sufficiently cleared for me to draw them, I spent my time in the Sety Temple, making fac-simile copies of the Coptic graffiti on its walls. Then, when it was possible to draw in the hypogeum, I set to work there, but it was entirely owing to Miss Hansard's kind help that I was able to secure drawings of all the sculpture that we uncovered (with one exception, the sloping passage), before they were silted up. I have to thank Miss Eckenstein also for her help in copying in fac-simile the Greek and Phoenician graffiti in the Sety Temple, which are published in this volume. My thanks are due also to many people for assistance in various ways, but particularly to Mr. Thompson and Dr. Walker for help in translating the hieroglyphic inscriptions, and to Mr. Griffith, Mr. Crum, and Mr. Milne for translating the hieratic, Coptic, and Greek graffiti.

I should like also to say that anything that is good in this book is due to Professor Petrie and to Mr. Griffith, to whom I owe all my knowledge of Egyptology.

In the previous season Mr. Caulfeild had partially cleared the long passage within the temenos wall; the passage itself had not been laid bare, but the great mass of sand had been removed, leaving a gigantic furrow like a natural ravine (PL. I. 1.). The method of constructing this great hypogeum rendered it comparatively easy to discover that there was building below, though the depth at which it lay made it impossible to clear more than a small portion. The nature of the desert is that after removing from two to four feet of loose wind-blown sand, the hard marl, called *gebel* by the workmen, comes into view. This is so firmly compacted together that it can be cut like rock. The ancient builders took advantage of this fact, and excavated passages and halls with steeply sloping, almost perpendicular, sides. These were lined and roofed with great blocks of stone, and the hollow at the top filled up with sand; the building was then completely hidden from the outside. In our clearance it was only necessary to descend a few feet till the rock-like *gebel* was exposed, and then to follow down the excavation; and the trial-pits that we sunk within the temenos invariably showed that the *gebel* had been cut perpendicularly to admit of building below. We spent three weeks in hunting for a place where the roof still appeared to remain, and were puzzled all the time at the number of right-angled turns which this extraordinary passage, as we then thought it, appeared to make. These turns, as we now know, must be the rock cuttings to hold chambers and halls. Finally we decided on a likely place, where the Roman rubbish, which had filled the part already cleared by Mr. Caulfeild, touched the clean marl filling of the desert. Here it was that we hoped to find the place where the roof was still intact. For days I carried candles and matches in my pocket ready to enter the passage as soon as there was a hole big enough to squeeze through; but they were never required. Throughout this excavation it was always the unexpected that happened; we expected to find a passage, we found chambers and halls; we expected to find it roofed in, the roof had been completely quarried away; we expected to find a tomb, we found a place of worship.

Our first deep pit brought us into the South Chamber, which gave us the cartouche of Merenptah, and made us realize that we had found a building which has no known counterpart in Egypt. Then came the discovery of the Great Hall and then of

B

the sloping passage. Here our hopes rose high, for the entrance to the passage had an enormous roofing stone still in position; but we soon found that it was the only one that remained, the rest of the roof having suffered the same fate as the other parts of the building. I was able to copy only a very small portion of the inscriptions; for though we cleared the passage to the floor, two days of high winds silted it up to the level of the roof. The whole of the excavation was greatly retarded by heavy falls of sand, the Roman filling being so loose that there were continual rivulets of sand running down the sides; and a high wind would bring down half a ton of sand and stones in one fall. To sit in a deep pit under an irregular but continuous fire of small stones, with the chance of a big stone coming down too, is an experience more amusing to look back upon than to endure.

At the north end of the north passage we started another excavation, for it was there, beyond the temenos wall, that the big marl heaps stood. It was partly by these heaps that Professor Petrie had deduced the fact that a large building lay below the surface of the desert. They were not natural heaps, and yet they were of clean marl unmixed with any remains left by man. They were too far from the temples of Sety and Rameses to have been the rubbish removed from their foundations; they were too large to be from the excavations of an ordinary tomb; and as the ancient Egyptian, like his modern descendants, never took unnecessary trouble, it follows that the tip-heap would be as near to the excavation as was allowable. Just inside the temenos wall, at a depth of about thirty feet, we came upon a vaulted passage of mud bricks which extended thirty-five feet northward, and was then apparently broken, for it was filled with sand. The thirty-five feet brought us to the north face outside the temenos wall, where we sank a large pit with this curious result:—

The rock-like *gebel*, at a distance of about sixty feet from the wall, was cut in a slope like a stair-case from the surface of the desert, sloping down towards the wall. Two mud-brick retaining walls had been built across it to hold back the sand.

At a distance of fifteen feet from the temenos wall, we found a square shaft (of which the wall formed one side), lined with mud bricks, some of which bore the cartouche of Sety I. The vaulted passage, which we had entered from the other side, ended in a small arch in the temenos wall, and its

floor was paved with blocks of stone. We reached a depth of over thirty feet, and came to undisturbed basal sand on which the walls rested. In the vaulted passage, the pavement was lifted, but with the same result—undisturbed basal sand. This was during the last days of the excavations, and there was no time to make further research. As to the meaning of this extraordinary shaft I can offer no explanation, nor can I even hazard a guess. The great marl heaps lead to the belief that there is still a large underground building at that end, though our efforts failed to find it.

2. This hypogeum appears to Professor Petrie to be the place Strabo mentions, usually called Strabo's Well. He describes it as being under the Memnonium; with low vaulted arches formed of a single stone, by which he probably meant that the stone beams went across the halls and chambers in a single span. Whether the entrance is really inside the Temple of Sety, thereby leading him to believe that it was under that building, or whether it was entered from the back door of the temple was not ascertained. As to the spring which he mentions, it might well be that already the lower parts of the hypogeum were then below high Nile level, and that what Strabo saw was the remains of the inundation, which he mistook for a natural spring.

3. At first sight there was nothing to indicate the real nature of this building, but later, two hypotheses presented themselves. The cartouche of Merenptah appeared in every place where it could be inserted, and we therefore had to consider the possibility of its being his tomb. The two points in favour of this hypothesis are that the walls are inscribed with scenes and chapters from the Books of Am Duat and of the Dead, and that Merenptah is called the Osiris and "Maat-kheru." Now M. Maspero has pointed out very clearly that the epithet Maat-kheru can be applied to the living equally well as to the dead; one of his most convincing instances being taken from the Temple of Sety at Abydos, where the youthful Rameses II, destined to live to a very great age, is called Maat-kheru. I have endeavoured to prove (chap. v.) that the king, in his lifetime as well as in death, was identified with Osiris; this being so, the fact of his being called Osiris does not of itself show that this was his funeral monument. We must remember also that Merenptah had a very fine tomb in the

Valley of the Kings; he was hardly likely to make two of such magnificence, one at Thebes and one at Abydos. The other hypothesis was that this was the building for the special worship of Osiris and the celebration of the Mysteries, and this appears to me to be the true explanation, for many reasons. Each reason may not be convincing in itself, but the accumulation of evidence goes to prove the case. There is no tomb even among the Tombs of the Kings that is like it in plan, none having the side chamber leading off the Great Hall. Then, again, no tomb has ever been found attached to a temple; the converse is often the case, I mean a temple attached to a tomb; but this, as far as we can judge, is a kind of extra chapel, a "hidden shrine," as the mythological texts express it, belonging to the temple. It is only to be expected that Osiris, one of the chief deities of Egypt, should have a special place of worship at Abydos, where he was identified with the local god. And that it should be a part of the temple dedicated to the worship of the dead, and which had special chambers set apart for the celebration of the Osirian mysteries is very natural likewise. The building lies immediately in the axis of the temple; a line drawn through the temple and the desert pylon to the Royal Tombs passes through the sloping passage and across the centre of the Great Hall. This is not the result of accident, the temple being older than the hypogeum, but shows that both were dedicated to the same worship. The sculptures in the Great Hall are the Vivification of Osiris by Horus, and the offering of incense by Merenptah; between the two sculptures is inscribed chapter cxlii. of the "Book of the Dead," the "Chapter of knowing the Names of Osiris." The other chapters of the "Book of the Dead" inscribed on the walls were pronounced by M. Maspero, when he saw them, to be the "Book of Osiris." The books of "Gates" and of "Am Duat," which are sculptured and painted on the North passage, were said by the ancient Egyptians to have had their origin in the decorations which Horus executed on the walls of the tomb of his father Osiris.

CHAPTER I.

THE SOUTH CHAMBER.

4. The chamber south of the Great Hall is sculptured on the east, south, and west walls with the clxviiith chapter of the "Book of the Dead." This is a rare chapter, being known only in three papyri, one in the Cairo Museum from the tomb of Amenhotep II, one in the British Museum (No. 10,478) of the XXth Dynasty, and one at St. Petersburg. This, however, is the only instance in sculpture of this chapter. The papyrus of Amenhotep II has been published in fac-simile without translation, the British Museum papyrus has been translated by Dr. Budge, but the vignettes are not published; and the St. Petersburg papyrus is still unpublished. In none of these papyri does the king appear, nor are the gods of the first seven *Qererts* mentioned.

5. At first sight the arrangement appears confused, but a closer examination shows a very definite order. The whole chapter is devoted to the worship of the gods of the twelve *Qererts* by the king. Each section contains a vertical line of inscription, reaching from the top of the wall to the bottom; this gives the numbers of the *Qererts*. On one side of each of these vertical inscriptions are three figures of the king kneeling and making an offering; above his head are three, four, or five short vertical lines of hieroglyphs. On the other side of the long vertical inscription are representations of the gods of each *Qerert*. These generally appear in three registers, corresponding with the figures of the king, thus the king makes an offering to every register. (In the description the registers are numbered 1, 2, 3, beginning at the top; the sections are indicated by Roman numerals.) The word *Qerert* in its literal sense is a Cavern, but it may here be taken, perhaps, to mean a Division of the night.

6. I. THE EAST WALL. PL. V.—Long vertical line of inscription: "The gods of the first *Qerert* in the Duat. The gods of the second *Qerert*. The gods of the third *Qerert*. The gods of the fourth *Qerert*. The gods of the fifth *Qerert*. The gods of the sixth *Qerert*."

On the left side of the inscription :—

1. The king kneeling and making an offering. Above him are five vertical lines of inscription: (1) " *Yu uden en sen ā tep ta.* There is offered to them a handful (measure of capacity) upon earth. (2) It is that the king Ba-en-Ra mer-Neteru, true of voice, (3) son of the Sun, his beloved, Hotep-her-Maat Merenptah, true of voice, (4) is as the lord of offerings in *Amentet* (5) and of cool water in [the Field] of Offerings."

2. The king kneeling and making an offering.

Above are five short lines of hieroglyphs: (1) "There is offered to them a *hin*-measure upon earth. (2) It is that the king Ba-en-Ra mer-Neteru, true of voice, (3) son of the Sun, Lord of Crowns, Hotep-her-Maat Merenptah, true of voice, (4) is as the lord of offerings in *Amentet*, (5) and of cool water in the Field [of Offerings]."

3. The king kneeling and making an offering. Above are five short lines of hieroglyphs: (1) "There is offered to them a *hin*-measure upon earth. (2) It is that the king Ba-en-Ra mer-Neteru, true of voice, (3) . . . . . . lord of Crowns, Hotep-her-Maat Merenptah, true of voice, (4) . . . . . . lord of offerings in *Amentet*, (5) . . . . in the Field [of Offerings]."

On the right-hand side of the long vertical line are the gods of the six *Qererts* enumerated in the inscription. In each *Qerert* there are three deities, male, female, male. Those of the first, third, and fifth *Qererts* are mummified figures; the others are represented as living.

II. The long vertical line of inscription reaching from the top of the wall to the bottom : "The gods of the eighth *Qerert*." Then comes a sentence with the hieroglyphs reversed : "Hail, O ye souls, weighing . . . . distinguishing righteousness from evil." A blank space, after which the hieroglyphs are written as at the top of the line : "The gods of the seventh *Qerert*." The reason that the two numbers, seven and eight, are in reverse order appears to be that the gods of the seventh *Qerert* are only three in number, like those immediately preceding, and that they can be fitted into the sculpture only in that particular place.

On the right is another vertical line of hieroglyphs reaching from the top of the wall to the bottom. The inscription is divided into three parts, which must be read in connection with the short lines of hieroglyphs above the figure of the king.

On the left of the long vertical inscription :

1. The king kneeling and making an offering. Above are three short lines of hieroglyphs. (From the long line :) "There is offered to them a handful upon earth from the Lord of offerings in *Amentet*, and of cool water in the Field of Offerings." (The short lines) (1) "It is that the king Ba-en-Ra mer-Ptah, true of voice, (2) is as Lord of offerings in *Amentet*, (3) and of cool water in the Field of Offerings."

2. The king kneeling and making an offering. Above are three short vertical lines of hieroglyphs.

(The long line :) "There is offered to them a handful upon earth when the chiefs of the living ones hear." (Short lines) (1) "There is offered to them a *hin*-measure upon earth. (2) It is that the king Ba-en-Ra mer-Neteru, true of voice, (3) is as the hearer (?) . . . of the living."

3. The king kneeling and making an offering. Above are three short vertical lines of hieroglyphs. (Long line) "There is offered to them a *hin*-measure upon earth. (Short lines) (1) "There is offered to them a *hin*-measure upon earth. (2) It is that the king Ba-en-Ra mer-Neteru, true of voice, (3) is as the hearer . . . . . . of the living."

On the right of the two long vertical inscriptions :—

1. Four men, each carrying a woman on his shoulder. *Fayu hert-sen*, "Those who carry their mistresses."

Four men, each carrying a man on his shoulder. *Fayu heru-sen*, "Those who carry their masters."

A vertical line of hieroglyphs : "There is offered to them a handful upon earth at the sacred pylon of *Neb Zat*."

Four women lying on their faces with their hair falling down. The papyrus of Amenhotep gives the word *Nenyu*, here shortened to *Nen*, "Those who give honour."

2. Three men and a woman lying on their faces, making offerings. They are called *K'heryu Autu*, "The possessors of food offerings." Below these are two men and two women lying on their faces, with outstretched hands. Mr. Griffith suggests that the hieroglyphs may read, "The smitten of Ra," and that what appears to be the loose hair falling over the face is really blood pouring down, as in the hieroglyphic sign for Death. This is a very probable explanation, as two of the figures are of men, for whom long hair would be quite inappropriate.

A vertical line of inscription: "There is offered to them a *hin*-measure upon earth, when the body lives in *Amentet*. There is offered to them upon earth from the follower of the great God at the secret door."

Four men bending down so that their hands touch the ground. The hieroglyphs are partially destroyed, but the name can be recovered from the papyrus of Amenhotep II, *Hefiu*, "The humble ones."

3. Four men supporting tall pillar-like objects. *Kheryu hotepu*, "The possessors of offerings."

III. A vertical line of inscription reaching from the top to the bottom of the wall: "The gods of the ninth *Qerert* in the Duat, secret of forms, cutting off the winds (?)."

On the left of the vertical inscription :—

1. The king kneeling and making an offering. Above are four short vertical lines of hieroglyphs : (1) "There is given to them a handful upon earth. (2) It is that the king Ba-en-Ra mer-Ptah, true of voice, (3) is as Lord of offerings in *Amentet* at the sacred pylon in *Neb-Zat*."

2. The king kneeling and making an offering. Above are four short vertical lines of hieroglyphs greatly defaced. (1) "There is . . . . upon earth. (2) It is that . . . . . true of voice, (3) son of the Sun, Lord of . . . . true of voice, when entering the secret places." The word *menu* is probably a scribe's blunder for *Shetau*.

3. The king kneeling and making an offering. Above are four short vertical lines of hieroglyphs : (1) "There is offered to them a *hin*-measure upon earth. (2) It is that the king Ba-en-Ra mer-Neteru, true of voice, (3) in entering the secret [places] in *Amentet*."

(PL. IV.) To the right of the vertical line :—

1. A god holding an *uas*-sceptre, his name is *Āhā*, "He who is firmly placed." A mummified figure called *Sheta*, "Secret." A bull and a uraeus on a stand ; the bull is called . . . *deg Asàr*, " . . . . Osiris." A mummified figure without a name. A bull and uraeus on a stand, he is called *Ymen-Asàr*, "Osiris is hidden." Below are two bulls with uraei on stands, and two mummified figures, alternately ; the first bull is *Ymen-Asàr*, "Osiris is hidden " ; the mummified figure is *Hāp;* the second bull is *Seshta Asàr*, "Making Osiris to be in secret." The mummified figure is called apparently *Sheth*.

Two short vertical lines of hieroglyphs : (1) "There is offered to them a handful upon earth, (2) from him who belongs to the eastern people in the Duat." Below these, though not exactly under them, are two more short vertical lines of hieroglyphs : (1) "There shall be offered to them a handful upon earth from him who belongs (2) to the eastern people in the Duat."

A crocodile-headed god holding an *uas*-sceptre and an *ankh;* behind him are four mummified figures. Unfortunately the inscription is so mutilated as to be illegible, and it cannot be restored from the papyrus of Amenhotep II.

Two vertical lines of inscription partially de-stroyed : (1) "[There is offered] to them a handful upon earth from a powerful one (2) . . . . every land, great of . . . . . . , chief of the Glorious Ones."

Four women kneeling on chairs ; the first letter of the name is broken away, and in the papyrus of Amenhotep it is almost illegible, it may, however, be S, for there is a word *Senen*, which means "Image," and here the name is *Senentyut*.

A jackal-headed god, with his name Anubis above him, holding a human-headed staff in each hand. In the papyrus of Amenhotep he holds two *heq*-signs.

In the row below are four mummified male figures. *Shetayu ā*, "Those who hide the hand" ; four mummified female figures, *Shetayut ā*, "Those who hide the hand." A god holding an *uas*-sceptre and an *ankh*, *Amen hāu*, "Hidden of limbs." Two vertical lines of hieroglyphs : (1) "There is offered to them a handful upon earth. It is that the king Ba-en-Ra mer-Neteru (2) is among the hearers who are upon earth."

Four birds, each sitting on a tree, *Bau peryu*, "The souls which go forth." Four mummified figures, *Aryu nehaut*, "Those who belong to the sycomore trees." Four men bending backwards, *Shesepyu*, "Those who bend (?)."

2 and 3. A vertical line of inscription ; the words are repeated twice : "There is given to them a *hin*-measure upon earth in entering the secret places."

Twelve figures of Osirified gods in shrines. The hieroglyphs read : "The gods who are in their shrines upon the sand." There is a curious curved line going from one side of the shrine to the other ; I take this to be an attempt to indicate that the inner part of the shrine itself was curved.

Two vertical lines of inscription reaching to the ground. There is only one sentence, repeated four times, showing that it applies to the four rows of figures who come next. Each sentence begins in the left-hand line and ends in the right-hand line ; it occupies exactly the same space as a single register of the gods to whom it applies : "There is offered to them a handful upon earth from a Glorious One who is in the secret place at the chamber (*āryt*) within the Duat."

Four rows of twelve figures, alternately male and female. The gods carry *uas*-sceptres and *ankhs;* of the goddesses, six carry the *ankh*, the rest are empty-handed. The hieroglyphs are the same in each row, *Neteru netertyu* (sic) *ymyu khet Asàr*, "The gods and goddesses who follow Osiris."

The carelessness of the sculptor is very well exemplified here; the base line of the third row of deities is still incomplete, a piece in the middle not having been incised.

7. PL. III. THE SOUTH WALL.—At the top is the winged disk with horns and pendant uraei. The wings are drooped so as to fit the gable of the pent-roof; nearly half the gable has been destroyed, but fortunately the name of Ba-en-Ra mer-Ptah, the throne name of Merenptah, still remains between the two uraei. To the left at the tip of the wing is the name Beḥdet, determined with the city sign. Under the curve of the wing are the words, " May he give the [sweet] breezes of life."

The whole wall is occupied with the inhabitants of the tenth *Qerert*. The inscription appears to begin as usual with the long vertical line which comes next to the king making offerings. "The gods of the tenth northern *Qerert* of the Duat, those who cry aloud, sacred of mysteries."

To the left of the long vertical inscription :—

1. The king, beardless, kneeling and making an offering. Above are four vertical lines of hieroglyphs : (1) There is offered to them one *hin*-measure upon earth. (2) It is that the king Ba-en-Ra mer-Ptah, true of voice, (3) [son of the Sun], his beloved, Hotep-her-Maat Merenptah, before the lords of eternity, (4) he who makes light in the secret places."

2. The king, bearded, kneeling and making an offering. Above are four vertical lines of inscrip-tion : (1) "There is offered (2) to them a handful upon earth. (3) It is that the king [Ba-en-Ra] mer-Neteru, true of voice, (4) is as lord of the offerings of food."

3. The king, beardless, kneeling and making an offering. Above are four vertical lines of inscrip-tion : (1) "There is offered (2) to them a handful upon earth. (3) It is that the king Ba-en-Ra mer-Neteru is as an excellent Glorious One in the Duat."

To the right is a long vertical line of inscription : " There is offered to them a *hin*-measure upon earth from him who makes light in the secret place repulsing the Sebyu-fiend on the day of . . . powerful in *Amentet*."

1. Two rows of four men standing. The name is almost destroyed.

Nine mummies laid upon biers. The hieroglyphs are *Pat sau ymyu.* " The whole body of the sons who

are within (?)." The word *Pat* is said by Dr. Budge to mean the "mass" (like a cake or dough), meaning " the whole body " ; e.g., *Pat neteru* would be " the whole body of the gods."

3. Thirty-one figures in a walking attitude, but lying horizontally ; they are in pairs, except those at the left-hand corner where there are three together. Above them is written *Bau kheperyu em Asár*, " The souls who become as Osiris."

A vertical line of inscription reaching from the top to the bottom of the wall : " When transformations are made in *Amentet*, his soul, let it go forth for its refreshment, those who are therein (i.e. in *Amentet*) let them praise Ra, when he goes forth upon earth."

1. Eight women holding in the left hand, which is raised above the head, an object which looks like a whip. In the tomb of Rameses VI the whip is replaced by a net, and in papyrus No. 10,478 of the British Museum the object is painted blue and appears like a hatchet-shaped vessel from which water is pouring. The name is almost entirely destroyed.

2. Eight men standing : " Those who belong to the Glorious One."

3. Eight mummified figures from whose mouths water is pouring. Their name is *Pat ymenu ā*, " The whole body of the hiders of the hand." Behind these stands a woman called Shent, who is probably the goddess Shenty. She is generally represented under the form of a cow, and it is in the chapels dedicated to her that some of the Osirian mysteries are celebrated.

8. PL. II. THE WEST WALL.—The eleventh *Qerert* is shown partly on PL. II, partly on PL. III. PL. II, a vertical line of inscription : " The gods of the eleventh northern *Qerert*. He that covers the fainting one, concealing [his] secret places."

On the right side of the long vertical inscription are three registers :—

(1) The king kneeling and making an offering. Above are four short lines of inscription : (1) " There is offered to them a handful upon earth. (2) It is that the king, Ba-en-Ra mer-Ptah, true of voice, (3) son of the Sun, Hotep-her-Maat Merenptah, before Osiris (?), is as a Glorious One in going and returning and coming forth unto the day."

2. The king kneeling and making an offering. Above are three short lines of inscription : (1) " There is offered to them (2) a handful upon earth. It is

that the king, the Lord of the earths, (3) Ba-en-Ra mer-Neteru, is true of voice before Osiris."

3. The king kneeling and making an offering. Above are three short lines of inscription : (1) "There is offered to them (2) a handful upon earth. It is that the king (3) Ba-en-Ra mer-Neteru, is true of voice before Osiris."

To the left : A vertical line of inscriptions reaching the whole height of the wall : " There is offered to them a handful upon earth from a Glorious One going in and going out unto the day. It is that the king Ba-en-Ra mer-Neteru, true of voice, makes transformation as his heart desires in the Underworld."

1. The god Yqeḥ standing and holding an *uas*-sceptre and an *ankh*.

Nine gods lying either on or beside serpents on biers. The name is *Pat ynïu-khet*, " The whole body of those who follow."

PL. III. A vertical line of inscription : " There is offered to them a handful upon earth from a soul who follows Ra." Nine figures lying on biers ; they are called *Pat ḥeq Yment*, " The whole body of the rulers of *Amentet*."

A vertical line of inscription : " There is offered to them a handful upon earth [when] entering the pylon of the Sacred Land." Three small registers : in the upper one are four men with their arms raised, they are called *Heknyu* " The Praisers." In the middle register are four men standing, who are called *Bau tā*, " The Souls (?) of the Earth." In the lowest register is a man standing holding an *uas*-sceptre and an *ankh* ; his name is *Ba Amentet*, " The Soul of *Amentet*." Behind him is a woman treading on a snake.

2. (PL. II). Nine jackals on stands of the shape that are always used for divinities. The name of these jackals is *Neteru resyu*, " The gods, the watchers." A vertical line of inscription which extends to the ground : " It is that the king Ba-en-Ra mer-Neteru, true of voice, son of the Sun, Lord of diadems, Hotep-her-Maat Merenptah, is true of voice before Osiris Khenti-Amentiu."

PL. III. Nine women lying on their faces with their hair falling down and their arms raised. The hieroglyphs read *Pat ykebyu*, " The whole body of mourners."

A man standing with raised hand in an attitude of declamation ; he is called *Nys-ta* (?), " Summoner of the earth." Below him is another standing figure holding an *uas*-sceptre ; his name is written merely

with the reed-leaf which reads Y, the determinatives are a statue and the papyrus roll.

3. (PL. II). A snake with a woman's head, called *Zesert-tep*, " Sacred of head " ; behind her are four mummified bearded figures, called " Those who are with the Sacred of head."

A snake named *Reny (Meheny* in the papyrus of Amenhotep), behind whom are four standing figures ·whose name I cannot translate.

(PL. III). Then comes the vertical inscription already translated above. After that there are nine figures of men in a curious bending attitude, with their faces turned upwards. Their title is *Pat Ymen Asâr*, " The whole body of the hidden of Osiris." Behind them is a standing mummified figure called *Hetem*, " Destroyed of face."

The last section consists of a vertical line of inscription reaching the whole height of the wall : " The gods of the twelfth northern *Qerert* in the Duat. The offerings of the gods."

To the right are three registers :—

1. The king kneeling and making an offering. Above are five vertical lines of inscription : (1) " There is offered to them a *ḥin*-measure upon earth. (2) It is that the king . . . . true of voice, (3) son of the Sun, Hotep-her . . . . the great god   . (4) in his going forth from *Amentet* (5) at all the gates belonging thereto."

2. The king kneeling and offering fruit and cakes. Above are four vertical lines of inscription : (1) " There is offered to (2) them a handful upon earth. It is that (3) the king Ba-en-[Ra] mer-Neteru, true of voice, (4) is as lord of offerings of food in the Underworld."

·3. The king kneeling and making an offering. Above are four vertical lines of inscription : (1) " There is offered to (2) them a handful upon earth. It is that (3) the king [Ba-en-Ra] mer-Neteru, true of voice, (4) is as . . . . in the Under-world."

To the left of the long vertical inscription are three registers.

1. Fourteen snakes arranged in four rows ; within the coils of each snake lies a human figure. Four mummified bearded figures stand side by side.

A vertical line of inscription : " There is offered to them a handful upon earth when he goes forth and enters unto *Amentet* at all the gates belonging thereto."

Two registers containing thirteen small figures in all. The figures are standing, and each holds an *uas*-sceptre, four hold an *ankh* also. The inscription reads: " The gods who are in the land of Duat."

A bearded figure standing holding an *uas*-sceptre. His name is *Maāt-ta*, " Truth of the earth " (?).

2. Eleven rams' heads on poles : " Those who are with those who are in heaven and the earths."

Two vertical lines of inscription : (1) " There is offered to them a handful upon earth. It is that (2) the King Ba-en-Ra mer-Neteru, true of voice, is as a Glorious One, powerful in his cooling."

Two registers each containing four standing figures : " The gods who are with the lord."

A bearded figure standing and holding an *uas*-sceptre and an *ankh*. His name is *Heri-ta* (?), " He who is on the earth."

3. Four men bowing. They are called *Yuutyu*, " The aged ones." Two vertical lines of inscription : (1) " The King Ba-en-Ra mer-Neteru, true of voice, when he enters and goes forth (2) from *Amentet* at all the gates belonging thereto."

Fourteen snakes arranged in three registers ; in the coils of each snake lies a human figure : *Neteru ymyu Mehen*, " The gods who are with, [or, in] the snake Mehen."

9. PL. VI. (see also PL. I.) THE NORTH WALL.—These inscriptions are on either side of the doorway, and each consists of four lines.

Left : (1) " Speech of the Son of the Sun, Lord of Crowns, Hotep-her-Maat Merenptah, true of voice. I come before thee, Lord of the Sacred Land, Osiris, Ruler of Eternity. I make what thy *ka* desires in the land of the living. (2) Speech of the king, Lord of the Two Lands, Ba-en-Ra mer-Neteru, true of voice. I come before thee, Lord of Eternity, Unnefer, son, of Nut. I make for thee offerings (?) very great. I know that which belongs to thy table of offerings (?) on account of it. (3) Speech of the Son of the Sun, Lord of Crowns, Hotep-her-Maat Merenptah, true of voice. I come before thee, Lord of Amentet, Osiris, great of soul in the Duat. I have driven out evil from the earth in order to satisfy thy heart every day. (4) Speech of the King, Lord of the Two Lands, Ba-en-Ra mer-Neteru, true of voice. I come before thee, Lord of the Underworld, Lord of Eternity (*nehch*), Ruler of the Dead. I increase for thy *ka* the offerings consisting of bread and beer, oxen and fowls."

Right : (1) " Speech of the Son of the Sun, Lord of Crowns, Hotep-her-Maat Merenptah, true of voice.

I come before thee, Osiris, Lord of Augert. I establish thy cycle in the cities of the nome. (2) Speech of the King, Lord of the Two Lands, Ba-en-Ra mer-Neteru, true of voice. I come before thee, Osiris, Lord of Deddu. I bring unto thee breath for thy nostril, life and strength for thy beautiful face. (3) . . . . Hotep-her-Maat Merenptah, true of voice. I come before thee, Osiris . . . . [I make] for thee sacrifices every day. I know that thou livest by means of them. (4) . . . . I (cast down) thy enemies under thee."

CHAPTER II.

THE GREAT HALL.

10. The Great Hall, the floor of which was more than forty feet below the surface of the desert, was fifteen feet wide, thirty-four feet long, and seventeen feet high. There were three doorways, one to the south, leading to the South Chamber ; one to the east, to the sloping passage ; one to the north, to the north passage. The North and South Walls were covered with inscriptions. The West Wall is divided into three parts vertically ; the portion to the left hand is filled with a colossal scene of the Vivification of Osiris ; the middle portion contains part of the Chapter of knowing the Names of Osiris ; the right hand portion is occupied with the figure of King Merenptah standing before a heaped-up table of offerings, and making an offering of incense. The wall had originally had a frieze of the *kheker* ornament painted in yellow, blue, green, and black.

THE EAST WALL of the hall had had the facing of stone quarried away in Roman times, so that any decoration, either sculpture or painting, which might have been there, had perished. The floor, as in the South Chamber and the passages, was paved with blocks of sandstone. The roofing stones must have stretched from wall to wall, the entire width of the hall, as there are no pillars or other means of support. It is easy to see how stones of such a size would impress the minds of visitors, and Strabo's surprise is not to be wondered at.

Above the scene of Osiris and Horus (PL. I.) are two rectangular holes for driving in the wedges by which the stones were split out of the walls by the Romans. From the weather stains and marks of bird droppings, it seems that the place must have stood open and roofless for many years, though it was filled up again in Roman times. Sufficient traces of colour remained on all the sculptures to show that the background was white, the hieroglyphs red and blue, and the figures of various colours. Many of the details were added in the painting and do not appear in the sculptures, as, for instance, the bracelets on the arms of Merenptah and the striped garments of the figures of gods in the lists on the West Wall.

11. PL. VII. At the south end of the hall the walls on either side of the doorway are engraved with chapters from the " Book of the Dead." The upper part of the wall is so broken that the inscription is too fragmentary to translate. One line only, on the left is intact. " Speech of the King, Lord of the Two Lands, Ba-en-Ra mer-Neteru, son of the Sun, Lord of crowns, Hotep-her-Maat Merenptah, giving life."

East side of the door : This inscription is part of chapter xliii, the Chapter of the Identification of Members. It is noticeable that the name of Sety I occurs in the first part of the inscription.

" [Chapter] of driving away the slaughterings which are made in Henenseten by the King Men-Maat-Ra, true of voice, Strong One of the White crown, Image of the gods. I am the Child, (*four times*). O [Abu-ur, thou sayest this] day, ' The Slaughter-block is prepared with what thou knowest, coming unto decay (?). I am Ra, establishing praises; I am · the great god within the tamarisk-tree, the twice beautiful One, more splendid than yesterday (?) (*four times*). I am Ra, establishing praises. I am going forth [when] this Ra goes forth.

" The hair of Osiris Ba-en·Ra mer-Neteru, [true] of voice, is as Nu.

" The face of Osiris Hotep-her-Maat Merenptah, [true] of voice, is as Ra.

" The two eyes of Osiris Ba-en-Ra mer-Neteru, [true] of voice, are as Hathor.

" The two ears of Osiris Hotep-her-Maat Merenptah, [true] of voice, are as Upuaut.

" The nose of Osiris Ba-en·Ra mer·Neteru, [true] of voice, is as Kenti-khas.

" The two lips of Osiris Hotep-her-Maat Merenptah, [true] of voice, are as Anubis.

" The teeth of Osiris Ba-en-Ra mer-Neteru, [true] of voice, are as Serkt.

" The neck of Osiris Hotep-her-Maat Merenptah, [true] of voice, is as Isis.

" [The two hands] of Osiris Ba-en-Ra mer-Neteru, [true] of voice, are as the Soul, the Lord of Deddu.

" The elbow of Osiris Ba-en-Ra mer-Neteru, true [of voice, is as the Lady of Sais].

" The backbone of Osiris Hotep-her-Maat Merenptah, true [of voice, is as Set].

" The phallus of Osiris Ba-en·Ra mer-Neteru, true of voice, is as Osiris.

" The flesh of Osiris Hotep-her-Maat Merenptah, true of voice, is as the Lords of Kher-aha.

" The trunk of Osiris Ba-en-Ra mer-Neteru, [true of voice], is as the Great One of Terror.

" The body and back of Osiris Hotep-her-Maat Merenptah, true of voice, are as Sekhet.

" The hinder parts of Osiris Ba-en-Ra mer-Neteru, true of voice, are as the Eye of Horus.

" The legs of Osiris Hotep-her-Maat Merenptah, true of voice, are as Nut.

" The feet of Osiris Ba-en-Ra mer-Neteru, true of voice, are as Ptah."

West side of the door : This is chapter clxxx of the " Book of the Dead," one of the many chapters of Coming forth by Day.

" [The Chapter] of Coming forth by Day, of praising Ra in the West of Heaven, of making praises to those who are in the Duat, of opening a road for the Soul which is in the Underworld, of causing that it may walk with wide strides in the Underworld, of making transformations as a living soul by the king Ba-en-Ra mer-Neteru, son of the Sun, Hotep-her-Maat Merenptah, true of voice. Hail, Ra, setting as Osiris with all his diadems. The glorious ones, the gods, the people of the West [i.e: the Dead], they praise him, the Image not (*sic*) unique of the secret places, the Holy Soul of Khenti-Amentiu (?), Unnefer, he exists unto eternity and everlasting. Beautiful is thy face in the Duat. Thy son Horus is satisfied concerning thee. He speaks [lit. commands] for thee the commanding words. Thou grantest that he may appear as thy pillar of the Duat. Those who are in the Duat and of the steps of heaven are bidden before thee (?) I am the guardian of the gate who walks behind Ra. I have offered offerings in the Fields of Aaru, I have made libations on earth and in the Fields of Aaru, weighing words like Thoth. Hail, O gods, O ancestors, O Ra, lead ye my soul as ye lead the begetter of mankind with you at the side of the soul of Khenti-Amentiu."

12. THE WEST WALL. On the left-hand side is
a scene of the Vivification of Osiris by Horus.
Osiris is enthroned within a shrine. The throne has
the usual decoration of horizontal lines, and in one
corner is a panel of water-plants tied to the symbol
of union, emblematic of the union of Upper and
Lower Egypt. The base of the shrine is decorated
with a border of *ankh* and *uas* alternately. Osiris
holds the crook, the scourge, and the *uas*, his usual
emblems. The face appears to have been worked
in stucco or plaster, which has fallen out. The
stone was probably faulty just in that place, and the
stucco was used to cover up the bad part. We
found stucco used in this way in several places; and
when the sculptures were in good repair and freshly
painted the join would not be noticed. In front of
Osiris are four little mummified figures standing on
a lotus flower with two leaves; these are the four
children of Horus, who are generally represented
before the enthroned Osiris. Above them in the
corner of the shrine is the sun's disk encircled by a
serpent from whose neck hangs an *ankh*. The
inscription over the head of Osiris reads: "Osiris
Khenti-Amentiu, Lord of Deddu, Ruler of Abydos."
In front of Osiris stands Horus wearing the double
crown and holding in both hands a long staff surmounted by an *ankh*, the sign of life. He holds
the *ankh* to the nostrils of Osiris in order that the
dead god may inhale life, and may live again. The
name of Horus is inscribed beside him; "Horus,
avenger of his father, son of Osiris."

On the undecorated portion of the wall, immediately below Horus, is the graffito of a foot (PL. XII)
with a Karian inscription beside it. It is just the
height at which a man, seated on the ground, could
rest his foot on the wall while marking out the shape.
This graffito shows that the building was used as a
place of pilgrimage in Greek times, pilgrims always
leaving incised footmarks at the shrines which they
visited. The roof of the Temple of Sety at Abydos
is covered with graffiti of footmarks, sometimes
with names as in this case, sometimes uninscribed.
Above the head of Horus, and also behind him,
are three registers of inscriptions, portions of chapter
clxxiii of the "Book of the Dead," the speeches of
Horus to his father Osiris. Each line begins with
the words "Speech. Hail O, Osiris, I am thy son
Horus," which I have omitted in the translation.

1st line.   1. "I come and I bring to thee life, stability,
                  and strength for thy beautiful face.

2. "I come, giving homage to thee with
    vessels of water.

3. "I come and I overthrow thine
    enemies upon earth.

4. "I come and I make thy sacrifices in
    the Nomes of the South and North.

5. "I come and I make provision for thy
    altar upon earth.

6. "I come and I make sacrifice of offer-
    ings upon it.

7. "I come and I lead captive for thee
    thy enemies as bulls.

8. "I come and I overthrow thy enemies
    in all the gates (?).

9. "I come and I smite down all evil
    that belongs to thee.

10. "I come and I slay what thou hast
     done when thou hast transgressed.

11. "I come and I destroy those who are
     hostile to thee.

12. "I come and I bring to thee the South,
     seizing all boundaries.

13. "I come and I bring to thee the
     companions of Set, chains (?) upon
     them.

14. "I come and I establish for thee divine
     offerings from the South and North.

2nd line.   1. "I come and I plough for thee the
                  fields.

2. "I come and I fill for thee the canals.

3. "I come and I build water channels
    for thee.

4. "I come and I bring thee cool water
    from Elephantine.

3rd line.   1. "I come and I cause that thou art
                  strong upon earth.

2. "I come and I cause that thou art
    glorious.

3. "I come and I cause that thou art
    terrible.

4. "I come and I grant to thee that Isis
    and Nephthys shall stablish thee."

PL. IX.—THE WEST WALL. *Register I.*

13. 1. Osiris Khenti-Amentiu. One of the chief
titles of Osiris as identified with Khenti Amentiu,
the western god, God of the Dead.

2. Horakhti, the Horizon-Horus. The Greek form
of the name is Harmakhis (Hor-em-akht), Horus in
the Horizon. Horus is here identified with the sun

which is worshipped when on the horizon, i.e., at its rising and setting. In the Dream-stele of Thothmes IV., the king is represented worshipping a sphinx which is called Hor-em-akht, and in the text of the stele the king relates how the god (who is called both Hor-em-akht and Horakhti), appears to him in a vision under the form of the Great Sphinx.

3. Nu, the Primaeval Waters. Nu is often represented in the Book of the Other World (Am-Duat) as a bearded man upholding the Barque of the Sun (PL. XIII).

4. Maat, Goddess of Truth, Righteousness, and Law. Her emblem is the ostrich feather which she wears on her head. In scenes of the Psychostasia, the heart of the dead man is weighed against the feather of Maat, while the figure of the goddess is often represented on the support of the balance to indicate the strict impartiality of the weighing. In mythological texts the gods are said to live upon Maat, and the words used make it appear that they actually ate Maat. This may account for the figures of the goddess of Truth, which are constantly offered to the gods by royal personages, together with offerings of food and clothing. Plutarch gives a curious corroboration of this when he says that on the feast of Hermes the Egyptians eat honey and figs, saying to each other at the same time, "How sweet is Truth."

5. The Boat of Ra. The Egyptians conceived of the sky and the other world as a more or less exact facsimile of the world and the country which they knew. As the Nile flowed through Egypt and formed the great highway, so a celestial river flowed through the sky and the Duat (the other world), and on this river sailed the great boat in which the sun made his daily journey from east to west, and at night followed the course of the river through the Duat. The Boat of the Sun is figured on scarabs as a charm, generally followed by the words *En send*, Fear not. M. Chassinat gives a translation of a curious magical ceremony to protect the Boat of the Sun. "Book of protecting the Divine Boat. To be said over the statuette of Set made of red wax, on the day of the voyage of the Boat to Abydos; after having bound it [the statuette] with hair of a black colour. Place a harpoon upon it, and wrap it in a fishing-net, the two arms having been cut off with a knife of black *tes ;* then put it on a fire with branches of *khasi* (cassia ?) under it." (CHASSINAT, *Rec. de Trav.* xvi. 114.)

6. Atum. One of the gods of Heliopolis, and generally identified with the setting sun. Ra, the sun-god, was worshipped as Khepra at his rising and Atum at his setting. The entrance to the sixth gate of the other world (PL. XIII) is decorated with two poles, surmounted by the heads of Khepra and Atum as symbolical of the position of the sun, which is then half-way between his setting and his rising, and therefore partakes of the characters of both deities.

7. The great cycle of the gods.

8. The little cycle of the gods.

Every great religious centre had its greater and lesser cycle or ennead of gods. In the Pyramid of Pepy II (*l.* 665), the great cycle of Heliopolis is said to consist of Atum, Shu, Tefnut, Geb, Nut, Osiris, Isis, Set, and Nephthys. In chap. xvii of the "Book of the Dead," Ra is said to create the cycle of the gods out of his own names: "I am Ra at his first appearance. I am the great god self-produced. His names together compose the company of the gods. Who then is this? It is Ra, as he creates the names of his limbs, which become the gods who accompany him."

9. Horus, Lord of the Urert Crown. The Urert or Double Crown is the emblem of sovereignty over the South and North. The semi-circular basket on which it is placed has the phonetic value *Neb*, "Lord," and appears in the *Nebti*-title of the King, where the Uraeus and Vulture, emblems of the goddesses of the South and North, are each figured upon this sign.

10. Shu. Shu uplifts the sky-goddess, Nut, from the embraces of the earth-god Geb. He is often mentioned in connection with the goddess Tefnut, and together they are called the Double-Lion deity.

11. Tefnut. The part which Tefnut plays in Egyptian mythology is not yet clearly defined. An inscription at Dendereh, of which Brugsch gives a translation (*Dict. géog.*, 212), implies that she was a foreign goddess :—" From the 28th of Tybi to the 1st of Mechir, [festival] of the voyage of this goddess [instituted] by Ra. It was celebrated for her when she arrived at Bukem to see the Nile of Egypt and the produce of the land of Egypt. When she appeared she turned her back on the country of the the Sati (Asia)." Brugsch identifies Bukem with the district lying between El Kab and the port of Berenice on the Red Sea. One of the great trade routes from the Red Sea to Egypt passed through this region, and the inscription implies that the

worship of Tefnut came by this road from Asia into Egypt.

12. Geb. The earth-god, husband of Nut, goddess of the sky, and father of Osiris. His usual title is *Erpa Neteru*, Hereditary Prince of the Gods.

13. Nut. The sky goddess, wife of Geb, and mother of five of the principal deities of Egypt. Plutarch relates a legend that Nut fell under the displeasure of Ra, the sun-god, who ordained that none of her children should be born on any day of any year. Thoth, however, who loved Nut, played dice with the moon and won from that luminary the seventieth part of every day; he added these fractions together, and so obtained five whole days, which he inserted into the calendar at the end of every year. These five days belonged to no year; and therefore by this device Nut was enabled to bring forth her children, Osiris on the first day, Horus on the second, Set on the third, Isis on the fourth, Nephthys on the fifth. No trace of this legend is found in any Egyptian writings, but the intercalary days were observed as the birthdays of the five children of Nut. This goddess is pictured raised on the hands of Shu, her limbs drooping so that her hands and feet touch the ground. She thus represents the vault of the sky; and, to carry on the imagery, she is covered with stars, and the sun and moon are also figured on her body. Other representations (PL. XIII) show her standing on the head of Osiris to receive the dying sun when he enters the other world. The sun is born anew of her every morning, and dies in her arms at night. She is often depicted on the inner side of the lid or on the floor of coffins and sarcophagi, sometimes as a stately woman without attributes (Sarcophagus of Sety I, pl. 16), sometimes as a black woman strewn with stars, her hands raised above her head, and the sun and moon pursuing their course along her body. Occasionally she is represented as a cow. (*Tomb of Sety I, M.A.F. Hypogées Roy. T. iv, pl. 17*.)

14. Isis. The myriad named, the greatest of all the goddesses of Egypt. She was the daughter of Geb and Nut, born on the third intercalary day, and was the sister and wife of Osiris, and the mother of Horus. Temples were built and mysteries were celebrated in her honour, and she was identified with all the goddesses of the Egyptian pantheon. The Greeks called her Demeter owing to the resemblance of ritual in the worship of the two goddesses. A common title of Isis is the Great One of Magic Spells, and she was looked upon, even to the latest heathen times, as supreme in magic. She revealed herself to her worshippers as Sirius, the Dog-star, the brightest star in the heavens, whose appearance at dawn heralds the coming of the inundation.

15. Nephthys. Daughter of Geb and Nut, born on the fourth intercalary day; the sister and wife of Set, and concubine of Osiris by whom she had one son, the jackal-god Anubis. She does not appear to have had a separate worship, but is almost invariably represented with her sister Isis, either mourning over the dead Osiris, or standing behind the throne of Osiris, the god of the Dead. When pictured as mourners, Nephthys stands at the head of the deceased, Isis at the foot where she can look upon the face of the dead. In the papyrus of the Lamentations of Isis and Nephthys, which, like many late texts, preserves much of the ancient ritual, directions are given for the proper recital of this hymn of the two sister-goddesses on the 25th day of the month Khoiak, which is one of the days sacred to Osiris. " When this is recited, the place [where one is] is holy in the extreme. Let it be seen or heard by no one, excepting by the principal Kher-heb and the Sem-priest. Two women, beautiful in their members, having been introduced, are made to sit down on the ground at the principal door of the Great Hall. [Then] the names of Isis and Nephthys are inscribed on their shoulders. Crystal vases [full] of water are placed in their right hands, loaves of bread made in Memphis in their left hands. Let them pay attention to the things done at the third hour of the day, and also at the eighth hour of the day. Cease not to recite this book at the hour of the ceremony." (DE HORRACK, *Rec. Past*, xii, 125.) The writer of the papyrus appears to have supposed the ceremony to be so familiar to his readers that he did not think it worth while to give any further details. In the calendar of the Sallier papyrus, three days in the year are devoted to the lamentations of Isis and Nephthys. On the 16th and the 17th of the month Athyr the mourning takes place at Abydos; the latter date is noticeable as being the same that Plutarch gives for the treacherous murder of Osiris. On 24th of Athyr there is an allusion to a joyful ceremony, " Procession of Isis and of Nephthys, who rejoice to see Unnefer triumphant." (CHABAS.)

16. House of the Kas of the Universal Lord.

17. The Storm of the Sky which raises the god.

18. The Hidden One, in her dwelling.

19. Khebt, the mummified form of the God.

20. The greatly beloved, with red hair.

21. The abundant in life, the veiled one.

22. Her whose name is powerful in her works.

These are the seven celestial cows who, with their bull and the four heavenly rudders are figured in chap. cxlviii of the "Book of the Dead," the Chapter of Providing Food. The name of the second cow, "Shentet-rest-neter" recalls that of the cow-goddess Shenty, in whose presence some of the ceremonies in honour of Osiris were performed (The translation of these names is from NAVILLE, *P.S.B.A.* xxiv, 313). For the goddess Shenty, see CAULFEILD, *Temple of the Kings*, pl. ix.

23. The Bull, the husband [of the cows].

24. The Leader of Heaven, opening [the gate] of the sun's disk. The beautiful rudder of the Eastern sky. In a papyrus of the XXth to the XXVth Dynasty (Paris, No. 173, WIEDEMANN, *P.S.B.A.*, xxii, 156) the four rudders are represented by four ships with red sails, carrying offerings to four towns, which stand for the four quarters of the compass. The ship of the East sails to Kher-aha (Babylon, near Memphis), and carries as an offering a libation jar with two jets of water.

25. Ra making light in the Two lands. The beautiful rudder of the Northern sky. The red-sailed ship travels to Busiris carrying linen as an offering.

26. The Shining One (?) in the Temple of the Sand. The beautiful rudder of the Western sky. The red-sailed ship goes to Memphis with offerings of fruit and cakes.

27. Sharp of face (?) of the Red Ones. The beautiful rudder of the Southern sky. The red-sailed ship journeys to Heliopolis with burning and smoking incense. Professor Wiedemann remarks that the different offerings carried by the ships may have some connection with the religious cult of each town.

28. Amset.

29. Hapi.

30. Duamutef.

31. Qebhsennuf.

These are the Genii of the dead, the children of Horus, the gods of the four cardinal points, under whose protection the internal organs of the dead were placed. Amset, human headed, guarded the stomach and large intestines; Hapi, ape-headed, guarded the small intestines; Duamutef, jackal-headed, guarded the lungs and heart; and Qebh-sennuf, hawk-headed, guarded the gall bladder.

The four genii often stand on a lotus which springs from the throne of Osiris in the Judgment scene, and small figures of them occur among the amulets placed on the mummy in the coffin. The so-called Canopic Jars, which contain the viscera of the deceased, have lids in the shape of the heads of these four deities. The internal organs of Osiris were preserved as holy relics in Upper Egypt, those called Amset in the Serapeum of the eleventh Nome, those called Duamutef at Siut in the Serapeum, of which the name was Het-hau-Neter, House of the Limbs (or members) of the God. Allusions to the four genii of the dead are innumerable in all mythological and funerary texts.

32. Shrine of the South.

33. Shrine of the North.

These two shrines are always mentioned together, and are probably merely emblematic of the two great centres of religious worship, one in Upper, the other in Lower, Egypt. Here the Shrine of the South has the form of a funereal coffer, but in the temple of Bubastis, where Osorkon II offers to the two shrines (NAVILLE, *Festival Hall*, pl. iv, *bis.*) it is the Shrine of the North which has this shape. If, as M. Naville thinks, it had some mystical significance, it is probable that one is the shrine of the living, the other of the dead, Osiris; in which case, the earlier text, this of Merenptah, has represented them correctly, Osiris being the living king in the north, the dead king in the south.

34. The Sektet Boat.

35. The Atet Boat.

These are the two boats of the Sun; in one he made his daily voyage across the sky from east to west, in the other he travelled through the Duat, or other world, during the night. The Egyptians themselves appear to have applied the names quite indifferently to either boat, so that it becomes impossible to distinguish them. They were known in the Old Kingdom, mention being made of them on the Palermo Stone in the reign of Nefer-ar-ka-Ra of the Vth Dynasty. There are constant allusions to them in the "Book of the Dead." Chapter cliii, the Chapter of Escaping from the Net, is ordered to be recited "on a figure of the deceased which is placed in a boat. Thou shalt put the Sektet boat on his right, and the Atet boat on his left. Offerings will be made to him of cakes, beer, and all good things on the day of the birth of Osiris " (NAVILLE).

36. Thoth. The scribe of the gods, the great magician, always represented with the head of an

ibis. It is Thoth who superintends the weighing of
the heart before the Judgment throne of Osiris,
writing down the record upon his tablets, and
introducing the dead who have been proved sinless
of Thoth is Fendy, He of the Nose, in allusion to
the great god of the dead. A common appellation
the long beak of the ibis.

37. The Gods of the South.

38. The Gods of the North.

39. The Gods of the West.

40. The Gods of the East.

An elaborate way of including all the gods. In
the "Book of the Dead," chap. xv, we read, "The
gods of the South and of the North, of the West and
of the East, praise thee [Ra]," and again, "the gods
of the South, the North, the West, and the East
have bound Apep." In the Pyramid texts, Unas
calls on "Gods of the West, gods of the East, gods
of the South, gods of the North. O, four kinds of
gods who enclose the four pure lands" (*Unas,*
l. 572).

41. The sitting gods. Renouf (*P.S.B.A.* xix,
p. 108, note 5) explains this attitude as the squatting
position in which so many Egyptian figures are
drawn. The gods who appear in this posture are
generally of inferior rank, the great gods are either
enthroned or standing.

42. The gods of the offerings of food. These are
the gods of the dead in whose name offerings were
made for the *Ka* of the deceased.

43. The Great House.

44. The House of Flame.

According to Renouf (*P.S.B.A.* xv, 69) every
Egyptian temple had a Great House and a House of
Flame, "as most sacred adyta at the extremity
opposite the entrance. The former occupied the
central position, like the Ladye-chapel in our
cathedrals, and the latter stood by the side of it."
The Papyrus of the Labyrinth says the House of
Flame "is the place where the lamp is lighted to
show the way to Osiris on his lake." I would
suggest that it was also the chapel in which the
sacred spark was kindled on the festival of Uag
(cf. *Inscriptions of Siut*).

45. The Road of the South.

46. The Road of the North.

47. The Road of the West.

48. The Road of the East.

On the sarcophagus of Beb of the VIth Dynasty
(PETRIE, *Dendereh,* pl. xxxvi, 13), sixteen mystic
roads are cited, four to each quarter of the compass,
but I know of no other mention of the sacred
Roads.

49. The gateways of the Duat.

50. The Secret Doors.

51. The guardian of the doors of the gateways of
the Duat.

Doors and gates had a special significance among
the Egyptians, particularly the gateways of the other
world or the Duat. Chapter cxlv of the "Book of
the Dead" is entirely devoted to giving the names
of the gates and their guardians, without which
knowledge the deceased could not attain to Osiris.
The "Book of Am-Duat" also carefully enumerates
the names of the gateways through which the sun
had to pass, and also the names of the guardians
and doorkeepers of each gate.

14. 1. *Register II.* Osiris Khenti-Amentiu, Lord
of Abydos. Under the name of Khenti-Amentiu, the
local god of Abydos, Osiris is worshipped as God of
the Dead. The chief centre of the cult was naturally at Abydos, the sacred city where the head of the
god was preserved as a holy relic. This head with
the long wig was the emblem of Osiris, and was
carried, raised on a long pole on a kind of litter, in
the solemn processions in the temple of Abydos. On
the walls of the Osiris chapel in the temple of Sety
at Abydos two representations of the Sacred Head
are shown; and in the back part of the temple, where
the mysteries were celebrated, there is a third representation. In all three cases the long, hanging wig,
made apparently of lazuli beads, is a prominent
feature. This makes it probable that the head
which was carried in processions was merely a
reliquary in which perhaps the relic was enclosed.
Professor Petrie has pointed out that the origin of
the name of Abydos is derived from this Sacred
Head. The hieroglyph which reads *ab,* and which
means emblem, is the head on a pole; the sign
which follows, *du,* means a hill; so the whole word
Abdu means The Hill of the Emblem. Osiris, who
was at one time the chief deity of Egypt, afterwards
fell from his high estate as the god of all goodness,
and became merely the spirit or demon by whom
enchanters worked magical spells; and the final
mention of him, under the name of Amente, in a
Coptic text, shows that he had reached the lowest
point of degradation. "Death came, Amente following him, who is the counsellor and the villain, the
devil from the beginning, many attendants of divers
aspects following him, all armed with fire, without

number, brimstone and smoke of fire coming forth from their mouth." (ROBINSON. *Copt. Apoc. Gospels*, p. 157.)

2. Osiris Unnefer, literally, the Good Being. One of the many names of Osiris, but which appears to have come into common use only in the XIXth Dynasty; from that time onwards it was the chief appellative of the god. This name greatly impressed the classical authors who write on the subject. Hermes Trismegistos (I quote from Ménard's translation) says, when speaking of Unnefer, "Dieu est le Bien et n'est pas autre chose. Dieu et le Bien sont une seule et même chose et le principe de toutes les autres. Dieu est le Bien et le Bien est Dieu. Le Bien agit par le moyen du soleil, le Bien est le principe créateur." Plutarch says, "Osiris is a good being; the word itself, among its various other significations, importing a benevolent and beneficent power, as does likewise that other name of Omphis [Onnofris, Unnefer], by which he is sometimes called." The word Unnefer has been noticed as still in use in our own times. It was the name of a Coptic saint; thence it passed to Spain under the form of San Onnofrio, after whom a town in Mexico was called, from which town the mineral "onofrite" takes its name.

3. Osiris, the Living One.

4. Osiris, Lord of Life.

In papyri which contain this chapter, these titles are, Ankhy, "The Living One," and Neb Ankh, "The Lord of Life." A difficulty here is that both these titles, which are almost entirely destroyed, begin with Ankh. There is no reason to suppose that the name Ankhy was twice repeated; it is almost certainly a mistake either of the scribe or the sculptor, one or both of whom were very careless, as the rest of the inscription shows.

5. Osiris-em-zer. A very common title of Osiris is Neb-er-zer, "Lord to the Boundary," i.e., The Universal Lord, of which this appears to be merely a variant.

6. Osiris, chief of the town of Pu. Here, again, is a mistake of the sculptor, for the papyri give Khenty (chief) instead of Khen. Pe, or Pu as it is written here, is the Buto of the Greeks, a very celebrated and holy city in the marshes of the Delta. It seems to have been a double town, part being called Pe and part Dep; or possibly the temple, and not the town, had the double name. The city was held sacred because it was there that Isis fled to bring up her son Horus after the death of Osiris.

Hidden in the midst of the marshes the mother and child were safe from the fury of their enemy Set, the murderer of Osiris, and it was in this secure retreat that Horus remained till he at last came forth as the "Avenger of his Father," to do battle with the Power of Evil.

7. Osiris Orion. From early times Osiris was identified with the constellation Orion. In the Pyramid texts Pepy says, "Osiris comes to thee as Orion, lord of wine, in the good festival of Uag; he to whom his mother said, 'Become flesh'; he to whom his father said, "Be conceived in heaven, be born in the Duat,' and who was conceived in heaven with Orion, who was born in the Duat with Orion

O Pepy, thou who art that great star which leans upon Orion, go in heaven with Orion, journey in the Duat with Osiris. . . . . . Pepy has come, and he honours Orion; he introduces Osiris in his place."

8. Osiris Sepa. This very curious epithet has a centipede as its proper determinative. It is the title of the mutilated Osiris whose body was torn to pieces. It is sometimes found with the determinative of the backbone, and is there often translated as "Relic." Brugsch (*Dict. géog.*, 190) quotes from a text, of which he gives neither date nor place, which mentions "the sceptre, the whip, and the glorious Sepa" (with the determinative of the backbone) as relics of Osiris.

9. Osiris in Tanent (see III, 6).

10. Osiris . . . . Meht-Ner. I cannot attempt to translate this title, which in other texts is given as Mehenet, but here it is quite distinctly . . . . . *meht-Ner*, with the determinative of a vulture.

11. Osiris, the Golden One (?) of Millions of Years.

12. Osiris, the Double Soul of the Image. The Saïte recension gives *Erpeti*, the Two Princesses, i.e. Isis and Nephthys, instead of *Erpet*, the Image.

13. Osiris-Ptah, Lord of Life. This is a common title of Ptah, who, as the triple god, Ptah-Sokar-Osiris, was the god of the resurrection as well as of death.

14. Osiris, Chief of Restau. The literal meaning of Restau is Mouth of the Passages, meaning the Grave. All gods of the dead bear this title.

15. Osiris, chief of [or, upon] the hill-country. As Egypt was essentially a flat country, all foreign lands were, in contradistinction, supposed to be hilly. This title therefore shows the dominion of Osiris over foreign countries.

16. Osiris Anzety. Mr. Griffith has given an

interesting explanation of this title (*P.S.B.A.* xxi, 278). "Anzeti means the god of the nome Auzet, just as Zehuti (Thoth) means the god of the nome Zehnt.   . Anzeti is therefore the figure of the anthropomorphic Osiris (Anzti) of Dedu . . . . Osiris of Dedu seems, from his headdress, to be a god of birth, or of renewed birth, while Osiris of Abydos (who always follows him in the funerary formulae) is of death. . . . . . In somewhat later times the figure of this Osiris is the regular determinative of Aty, 'ruling prince,' a term applied only to the living being. . . . . Osiris of Dedu is the living king and a god of birth or generation, presiding over the nomes of the East, or Sunrise, while Osiris of Abydos is the dead King and King of the Dead, chief of the Westerners in the region of the Sunset."

17. Osiris in Sebet. In other texts this name is given as Hesert, a sanctuary in Hermopolis Magna. In the time of Rameses III there was a secret shrine (*kara sheta*), dedicated to the worship of Osiris, in the temple of Thoth in this place.

18. Osiris in Siut. Siut, the Lycopolis of the Greeks, was the centre of the worship of the jackal-god, Upuaut, who was identified with Osiris.

19. Osiris in Uzeft. Here is another mistake of the scribe or sculptor. The word should be Nezeft, a town in the Sethroïte nome not far from Pithom.

20. Osiris in the South. This word is undoubtedly spelt Res, which means the South, and it is the same in all the papyri; but it is very probable that in very early versions of this chapter it was read Nekhen, for the title which follows is Osiris of Pe, Pe being the religious capital of the North, Nekhen of the South. The names of the two towns are constantly used thus in juxtaposition when the writer wishes to express North and South. The sign for Nekhen, a plant with two leaves at the base, is very like the hieroglyph for South, the same plant with four leaves at the base, so it is not unnatural that the two should be confused, especially as the meaning is practically the same in this connection. In the early hieroglyphs indeed no difference is made between the two signs. If this were the South we should expect Osiris of the North to follow immediately after, but in all papyri Osiris of the South and Osiris of the North have been mentioned already.

21. Osiris in Pe. We have already had a mention of Pe, the city of Isis in the marshes, but there it is in opposition to Dep, which occurs further on, here it is opposed to Nekhen. The two temples, one in Pe and one in Dep, were dedicated, the one to Horus, the other to Uazt. Chap. cxii of the "Book of the Dead" is concerned with the Spirits of Pe, who are Horus, Amset and Hapi; chap. cxiii gives the Spirits of. Nekhen as Horus, Duamutef, and Qebhsennuf. In the Temple of Sety at Abydos, the Spirits of Pe and Nekhen carry the king on a litter, and at Bubastis the Spirits of both places are in attitudes of praise. The Spirits of Pe are hawk-headed, those of Nekhen jackal-headed.

22. Osiris in Neteru. Neteru is identified by Brugsch with Iseum, the modern Behbeit, a place specially devoted to the worship of Isis, and through her to Osiris. Neteru is often determined with the sign of a pool of water, and in the Pyramid texts it is mentioned in connection with a lake. "Pepy has washed himself in the four vessels filled at the divine Lake which is in Neteru" (l. 334).

23. Osiris in Lower Sais. The town of Sais, which was sacred to the goddess Neith, was divided into Upper and Lower, hence it is often called the Town of the North and South. In Sais, Osiris bears the same name as at Busiris, Anzety, the Living God.

24. Osiris in the town of the Double god. The hawk sign being an ancient symbol for God, this name probably means the town of Horus and Set, which might mean the king, one of whose titles in the early dynasties was Horus and Set. A tradition connects Aphroditopolis with the god Set, who is said to have been buried there. The name of the nome, in which Aphroditopolis stands, is written with the double hawk, the town itself being written with the determinative of two fingers or two sandals.

25. Osiris in Syene. We have here the cult of Osiris at the most southerly point of Egypt. Plutarch mentions Philae as a place specially sacred to Osiris, and the Ptolemaic ritual inscribed in the temple at Dendereh gives directions for the Osiris-worship at Elephantine. The temple at Philae itself preserves—or perhaps I ought to say, did preserve—inscriptions showing that so late as the Roman period, the worship of Osiris played a large part in the religious life of the place.

26. Osiris at the Mouth of the Canal, i.e. Illahun. Osiris had a special worship in the Fayum, and his most celebrated temple was at Illahun. As god of the Fayum he is identified with Sebek and is depicted as a crocodile, as on the sarcophagus of Ankhrui, which was found at Hawara in the Fayum (PETRIE, *Hawara*, pl. ii, p. 21.) where there is a picture of

the local Osiris, represented as a human-headed crocodile. The inscription reads, "Says Osiris of many aspects, O Osirian prince Ankhrui, hidden art thou in the great place of concealment on the west of the lake, which thou rejoinest morning and evening, living for ever." Mr. Griffith considers that the deceased is here "identified with the Osiris-crocodile daily plunging in the lake." In the Dendereh ritual, water from Illahun was used in the Osirian ceremony at Neteru. Osiris being to some extent a water-god, it is only natural to find his temples near a lake, as at Neteru and Illahun.

27. Osiris in Aper. This place, which appears to mean "Town of Provisions," is not yet identified. In the "Lamentations of Isis and Nephthys," it appears to be near Sais, for Nephthys calls on Osiris, "O god An, come to Sais. . . . Come to Aper; thou wilt see thy mother Neith " (*Records of the Past,* ii, 123).

28. Osiris in Qefnu, or Qefdenu in other texts.

29. Osiris Sokar in the Town of Pedu-sha. Osiris, the anthropomorphic god of the dead, was identified both with Ptah and with the hawk-headed Sokar; the three together forming the triple god, Ptah-Sokar-Osiris. The dominion of Sokar is given in the 4th and 5th divisions of the "Book of Am Duat," but M. Jequier shows that the dominion of Sokar was originally quite distinct from that of Osiris, and that the two have been incorporated together in the "Book of Am Duat" by later theologians. The Papyrus of the Labyrinth shows a connection between the two gods: "This place, the temple of the god Sokar, at the mouth of the canal (Illahun), is the town of Pi-bi-n-usiri (House of the Soul of Osiris). When he enters the Great Green (the Lake) to see Osiris in his lake, towards the south side of the canal, he rests at Heracleopolis Magna and at Hermopolis Magna equally." (BRUGSCH, *Dict. géog.* 169.)

30. Osiris, chief of his town.

31. Osiris in Pegasu-re.

32. Osiris in his places in the North Land. It is unusual to have the North put first.

33. Osiris in his places in the South Land.

34. Osiris in heaven.
35. Osiris in earth.

} The older papyri give only Osiris in the North, and Osiris in heaven, ignoring both the South and the earth.

36. Osiris in his places in the Mouth of the Passages.

37. Osiris of the Two Great Ones. This probably refers to the sister goddesses Isis and Nephthys.

38. Osiris of Atef-ur. A place near Memphis.

39. Osiris Sokar. In the temple of Sety at Abydos one part of the building is dedicated to Sokar. Twelve of the titles which he bears there are the same as those of Osiris in this inscription, Nos. ii, 27, 28, 29, 32, 33, iii, 5, 6, 14, 15, 18, 37 41. (MARIETTE, *Abydos,* i, pl. 48a.)

40. Osiris, Ruler of Eternity. This is one of the most frequent titles of Osiris, by which he is constantly called in the "Book of the Dead" and in funerary stelae.

41. Osiris the Begetter. In certain aspects, Osiris is supposed to be the creator of all living creatures, the begetter of mankind.

42. Osiris of Agenu.

43. Osiris of the Makes sceptre.

44. Osiris, Ruler of the Underworld. This region, Khertneter, is not the same as the Duat, or Other World, into which the sun entered in the evening and through which he travelled during the night.

45. Osiris, creator of all things.

46. Osiris, the good inheritor.

47. Osiris, Lord of the Sacred Land. Ta-zeser, literally translated as the Sacred Land, is a name for the cemetery. All gods of the dead, therefore, bear this title.

48. Osiris, Lord of Eternity. What the exact shade of difference is between Heq Zet (Ruler of Eternity) and Neb Zet (Lord of Eternity) is not known, but evidently a slight distinction was recognized, as this title, presumably a higher one, is used twice in this inscription, in which only a selection is given of the innumerable names of Osiris.

49. Osiris, King of Everlastingness. Here is a similar title to the preceding. Seten heh (King of Everlastingness) probably conveyed a different idea from both Heq Zet and Neb Zet to the Egyptians, though to us the words Eternity and Everlastingness, by which we translate Zet and Heh, have the same meaning. The two words Zet and Heh may have the meaning of "Eternity" and "Before Time," the distinction between which was one of the chief points in the Arian controversy in the fourth century.

50. Osiris, eldest of the five gods. The meaning of this title is quite obvious on referring to the legend of Nut, Osiris being the first of the five gods who were born on the intercalary days. The name is rather rare, but is known from the VIth Dynasty.

D

51. Osiris in the Hall of Truth of the Lord of the Two Lands, Ba-en-Ra mer-Neteru, i.e. Merenptah. M. Maspero says that the Hall or Place of Truth was the name of the Theban necropolis (*Catalogue du Musée égyptien de Marseille*, pp. 4 and 24), where the great ancestress of the XVIIIth Dynasty, Aahmes Nefertari, was buried. In that instance however the name, Hall of Truth, stands alone, here it is specially called the Hall of Truth of King Merenptah which makes it appear that the reference is to the Judgment Hall either of the King, or of Osiris.

15. *Register III.* 1. Osiris, Lord of Eternity.

2. Osiris Aty. Another form of the name Anzety (*q.v.*). Mr. Griffith (*P.S.B.A.* xxi, 278) says, " This word Aty (spelt with two crocodiles) may indicate that the god was sometimes in crocodile form, or at least connected with crocodiles." In quite late and Ptolemaic times, this title is applied to Osiris of the Fayum (PETRIE, *Hawara*, pl. ii, *Kahun*, pl. xxv).

3. Osiris Thetaty.

4. Osiris, Lord of the Tomb (see II, 14). Re-stau is literally the Mouth of the Passages, an appropriate name for pyramids and rock-tombs whose passages extend to so great a distance.

5. Osiris upon the Sand. It is very tempting to translate this as Osiris of the Bedawin (*Heriu Sha*) instead of Upon the Sand (*Her Shau*), but other texts give *Her-shau-ef* (Upon his Sand) as a well-known title of both Osiris and Sokar.

6. Osiris in Thanent. Probably the same as II, 9. Brugsch supposes it to be near Memphis. In chapter xvii of the " Book of the Dead," we find that "he to whom saffron cakes are brought in Tanent is Osiris."

7. Osiris in the hall of the [sacred] cows. Cattle of every kind were largely included in the cult of both Isis and Osiris; the cows being specially sacred to Isis, the bulls, particularly the bull Apis, to Osiris. The Serapeum of the Libyan Nome was called The House of the Cow.

8. Osiris in Nezyt, or Nedbyt in other texts.

9. Osiris in Sati (?). The word is partially obliterated.

10. Osiris in Bedesht.

11. Osiris in Depu. The sanctuary which, with Pe, is in the town of Buto.

12. Osiris in Upper Sais (see II, 23). A relic of Osiris was preserved in this town.

13. Osiris in Nept. An unknown place, generally written Nepert.

14. Osiris in Shennut.

15. Osiris in Henket. The Town of Offerings is not known except in this chapter of the " Book of the Dead."

16. Osiris in the Land of Sokar.

17. Osiris in Shau.

18. Osiris in the Town of Fat-Hor. This curious name, which means The Carrying of Horus, is probably given to some town where the carrying of the god formed part of the ritual.

19. Osiris in the Two Places of Truth. The duality of Maat or Truth is always insisted on in Egyptian religious literature. The Hall of Judgment, where the heart of the deceased was weighed before Osiris, is named the Hall of the Two Truths, or the Double Hall of Truth.

20. Osiris in Han.

21. Osiris in the Town of the Soul of his Father.

22. Osiris in the Mehent house.

23. Osiris, Lord of Eternity.

24. Osiris, in the Town of a Great Wind (Nif-ur). A name for Abydos. Osiris is always connected with the North wind, one of the usual funerary formulae is that he may grant to the deceased " the sweet breezes of the North wind," and in chapter clxi. of the " Book of the Dead," which speaks of the four entrances to heaven, that of the North wind is said to belong to Osiris. The name of the town, however, is probably due to its position, which is exposed to every breath of air from the North. Dr. Walker has suggested that the sail-sign should be read Ta unless it is actually spelt out as Nif, and that it interchanges with the sign for land. Therefore he would read this name Ta-ur instead of Nif-ur. This view is borne out by the spelling of Ta-ur in the inscription on the north wall of the great Hall (PL. XI).

25. Osiris in the Town of Tena. The word Tena, with the same determinative, is the name of two moondays. One, or perhaps both, are sacred to Osiris, and were specially observed at Abydos.

26. Osiris in the Town of Asheru. A place at Karnak, of which Mut was the great goddess.

27. Osiris in all Lands.

28. Osiris in the House of the Pyramidion. One of the holiest places in the temple of Ra at Heliopolis, to whose honour all obelisks, and particularly the pyramidion on the top, were dedicated.

29. Osiris in the Great House. Another name for the great temple at Heliopolis.

30. Osiris, Lord of Dadu, Upuaut of the North.

The identification of Osiris and Upuaut is proved by many passages in the "Book of the Dead." At Abydos (PETRIE, *Abydos* ii) Upuaut was evidently the original god, but was afterwards completely superseded by Osiris.

31. Osiris, the living Prince in the Land of the Lake, i.e. the Fayum (see III, 2).

32. Osiris, Lord of might, smiting the fiend. The Sebau fiend figures largely in the "Book of the Dead" as the enemy of Osiris, and therefore of the dead in general. "The Sebau fiend hath fallen to the ground, his arms and hands have been hacked off, and the knife hath severed the joints of his body.". According to Dr. Erman, it was Osiris of Memphis who conquered the enemy; "thine image is that which is seen at Memphis when thine enemy falls under thy [sandals]" (*A.Z.* 1900, p. 35).

33. Osiris Hershefi in Henen-Seten.· Hershefi, or Arsaphes in the Greek form, was identified with Osiris from the XIIth Dynasty, and perhaps earlier. He is generally figured with a ram's head, and wearing the head-dress of Osiris, and the horns are so marked a feature that the name of Osiris Hershefi is The Horned One. The name of his temple is *An-rud-ef*, The Place where nothing Grows. M. Naville (*Ahnas and Paheri*, p. 7) gives some interesting derivations of the name Hershefi. The name of the town itself appears to have been contracted from Henen-Seten to Henensi, in which form it appears in the list of Assurbanipal. In Coptic, it is still further contracted to Henes; and the modern Egyptians, by placing a vowel before the aspirate, have altered it to its present form of Ehnasya.

34. Osiris, the Bull in Egypt. Here again we have the identification of Osiris with the Bull, an identification which is most clearly seen in the worship of Apis. Osiris is constantly called the Bull of the West, i.e. the region of the dead; and at Bekhent, a town of Lower Egypt, he appears to have been called the Bull without any further title.

35. Osiris Nepra, Upuaut of the South. This is the most interesting of all the epithets applied to Osiris, but in these short notes it is impossible to discuss it fully (*vid. inf.* Osiris, in the Sed-festival). Nepra is the god of ripe corn, with whom Osiris, in his character of god of vegetation, is naturally identified. As early as the beginning of the Middle Kingdom he received this title (*Coffin of Amamu*, pl. xxvii), and it occurs also in that storehouse of mythology, the Book of the Dead.

36. Osiris in all his appearings. The manifes-

tations of Osiris were so numerous that his worshippers could never feel sure that they had not overlooked some in a list of this kind. It was therefore safer to end the list with a few epithets which would cover all omissions and so avert the anger which the god might feel at any neglect.

37. Osiris in all his houses of Long Duration. Brugsch in his dictionary gives this word *ahat*, determined with the sign of a house, as an equivalent for tomb or grave. The title would then read Osiris in all his Tombs.

38. Osiris in [or, with] all his ornamentations.

39. Osiris in all his incarnations (births).

40. Osiris in all his actions.

41. Osiris in all his names. The extraordinary attempt at archaic spelling in this epithet is worth noticing.

42. Osiris in all his places.

43. Osiris in every place in which his *ka* desires to be.

44. Osiris, chief of the gods.

45. Osiris, Ruler of the cycle of the gods.

46. Osiris, the great One of Eternity.

47. Osiris, eldest son of his Father.

48. Osiris, the Soul of the Gods. The souls of the gods are greatly confused in the Book of the Dead. Osiris is said to have a soul of his own as well as being the soul of other gods. In chapter xvii we find, "I am he whose soul resideth in a pair of gods. What then is this? It is Osiris when he goeth into Deddu and findeth the soul of Ra; there the one god embraceth the other, and becometh Two Souls."

49. Osiris, Ruler of the Underworld.

50. Osiris, King of Amentet, i.e. the West, or Region of the Dead. Amentet means Hidden, and is the epithet applied to the place in which the sun is hidden from his worshippers. As he was supposed to die when he left the earth, the hidden place into which he entered became the region to which the faithful went at death.

51. Osiris within the house of Ba-en-Ra Mer-Neteru.

16. On the right of the wall is a figure of Merenptah standing before a table of offerings. In front of him is a small altar inscribed with his name and titles. The table of offerings is in three registers corresponding to the three registers which contain the divine names. Among the offerings are the different joints into which the sacrificed ox is divided,

the head, leg, ribs, heart, and even the whole carcase, are represented.

The king holds a hawk-headed incense-burner; the small pottery saucer, which held the burning incense, is clearly shown. These saucers were used in order to save the bronze burner from contact with the fire, by which it would soon have been destroyed. Saucers of this kind, blackened inside, with charcoal and incense, were found by Prof. Petrie at Tel el Amarna. The bracelets on the king's arms are merely painted, not sculptured; an omission which would not have been noticed when the whole figure was coloured. The necklace is of a somewhat unusual form.

Above the head of the king is a hawk with outstretched drooping wings, on one side of it is the name, "Behdeti, lord of heaven;" on the other side, "He gives all life like Ra." Over the king are his name and titles, "The good god, son of Osiris, Lord of the Two Lands, Ba-en-Ra mer-Neteru, lord of crowns, Hotep-her-Maat Merenptah, giving life like Ra."

In front of Merenptah is an inscription, "Offering incense to all the fathers, the gods." Behind the king is, "Protection, life, stability, length of days, all health, all gladness of heart behind him, like Ra for ever."

17. PL. XI. THE NORTH WALL.—These inscriptions are portions of chapter cxlvi of the "Book of the Dead," the Chapter of the Hidden Pylons.

Right: "[Call aloud] O Osiris King Ba-en-Ra mer-Neteru, true of voice, on arriving at the first pylon, the Lord of Tremblings, [Lofty] of Walls, Lady of Overthrowings, arranging Words, repulsing storms, preventing injuries [to him who] goes along the road. Its doorkeeper, Nery is his name. Says the Osiris the King Ba-en-Ra mer-Neteru, true of voice: [Behold] me, I come. Says this guardian of the gate, saying: What says the Osiris the King . . . Verily, he being pure I am pure. How? [By] these waters in which Ra purified himself when he was clothed [on] the east of heaven. Thou art anointed. How? [With] *merhet, hati* and *ash* ointments, and the clothing which is upon thee . . . and the staff which is in thy hand is . . . . . . Pass thou on."

Below is a shrine in which is the vulture-headed deity Nery, wearing two feathers on the head, and holding the *ankh.* On the top of the shrine is a decoration of alternate feathers and snakes.

Left : "Call aloud, O Osiris King Ba-en-Ra mer-Neteru, true of voice, at the second pylon, the Lady of Heaven, Mistress of the Two Lands, Neby, Mistress of the Sacred Land. The name of its guardian is Mes-ptah-peh. He says, I made a road. Behold me, I come, saying: What says the Osiris, the King Ba-en-Ra mer-Neteru, lord of crowns, Hotep her-Maat Merenptah, true of voice? Verily, thou being purified I am purified. How? [By] these waters in which Osiris purified himself when he was placed in the Sektet boat and the Atet boat. He went forth at Ta-ur, he descended upon him who is in Ta-ur. Thou art anointed. How? [With] ointment and with perfumes of the festivals, and the clothing which is upon thee, and may there be bandages to thee. The staff in thy hand is thy *benben* staff. It is proclaimed for thee because thou knowest it, viz. the name of Osiris the King Ba-en-Ra mer-Neteru, son of the Sun, of his body, his beloved, lord of crowns, Hotep-her-Maat Merenptah, true of voice before the Lords of Eternity."

Below the inscription is a representation of a shrine containing a crocodile-headed figure wearing two feathers on the head and holding the sign of life. The name is Neby, determined with the sign of fire. Along the top of the shrine is a looped snake.

CHAPTER III.

THE PASSAGES.

18. PL. XII. The sloping passage leading from the hall towards the Temple of Sety was inscribed on the South side with the xviith chapter, on the North side with the xcixth chapter, of the Book of the Dead. Above the inscription on each side was a frieze of figures of which it was possible to copy only one, from the north side. The rapid silting up of the passage by heavy falls of sand and stones made it impossible to copy more than a few lines of the inscriptions, which are only enough to show the chapters from which they are taken.

The xcixth chapter is the Chapter of bringing the Makhent boat; the xviith is one of the most ancient chapters, of which the meaning was so obscure, even in the earliest times of which we have any knowledge of it, that it is accompanied by a running commentary by ancient theologians. By degrees, the commentary became confounded with the text, which then required a fresh commentary. In Renouf's translation (*P.S.B.A.*) the original text, so far as it can be ascertained, and the commentaries, are printed in different type, enabling the reader to distinguish between them at a glance.

The lintel or roofing stone, which still remains in position, was painted in black on a grey ground. It was probably the intention of the builders to engrave the hieroglyphs, but it was left, like the east side of the North passage, merely sketched in.

The names, which are determined with the sign of a star, are those of the dekans, and are interesting as none have hitherto been found of the time of Merenptah. The earliest known are in the tomb of Sety I, and in the Ramesseum of the reign of Rameses II; these now continue the consecutive series for another reign.

The whole roof of the passage was probably covered with the names of stars, and possibly with astronomical data, of which not a vestige remains except this one small section.

19. PL. XIII. The passage leading northwards out of the hall is sculptured and painted with scenes from the "Book of Gates."

On the East wall is the representation of the sunrise, on the West wall is the sunset. The latter was considered more important, for the West wall is sculptured, the East wall being merely painted.

Surrounding the whole scene is the pathway of the sun, with the disk of the sun placed half-way. The disk has been painted red, and was scribbled over with a half-legible Greek graffito.

The first scene shows the Boat of the Sun upheld by Nu, the primaeval Waters. The hieroglyphs explain that "These two arms go forth from the water; they raise this god." In the centre of the boat is the beetle, emblem of the resurrection, supporting the sun's disk. On either side are Isis and Nephthys, whose headdresses are the hieroglyphs which form their names; towards the stern of the boat and behind Isis, are five divinities, Geb, Shu, Heka, Hu, and one unnamed; the two last manage the great oars by which the boat is steered. Above is the sentence "The god [?gods] of the Atet-boat following this god [when he] sets." On the other side of the beetle, and behind Nephthys, are three gods named Sa. Above them are the words, "Those who are with him." In the prow kneels the king with upraised hands in an attitude of worship, with his name and titles above his head, "Lord of the Two Lands, Ba-en-Ra mer-Ptah, true of voice." This is the only instance I know of the king appearing in the boat of the immortals.

Over the boat is a straight line, above which are two figures upside down. The upper one is represented with the feet turned back till they almost touch the head. According to the hieroglyphs this is "Osiris encircling the Duat;" the Duat being the other World through which the sun passed at night. Osiris with raised arms supports the goddess Nut on his head. The hieroglyphs beside her read, "Nut receiving Ra;" the theory being that the sun was born of Nut every morning, and died in her arms every evening.

This scene of the circular Osiris is very rare; it occurs on the sarcophagus of Sety I and in the tomb of Rameses VI. The explanation of the peculiar position appears to me quite simple; the straight line above the boat I take to be the line of the horizon, Osiris and Nut being below the horizon. It was impossible to represent both sides of the horizon on an upright wall without having some of the figures wrong way up. The artist was forced to sacrifice truth to the exigencies of the case; the boat and its passengers, being the most important, are placed correctly, therefore Osiris and Nut, who are merely subordinate characters, are reversed.

The sunset is separated from the next scene by five lines of hieroglyphs. In the line nearest the boat are two serpents; the one at the top is upside down, and wears the head-dress of Isis; that at the bottom wears the head-dress of Nephthys.

The inscription between the two reads, "They are the guard of the secret gate of the souls who are in *Amentet*, after entering this gate."

Between the other lines of hieroglyphs are two serpents standing on their tails, the one called *Sbay*, "He of the gate" [or perhaps *Duay*, "He who praises"], the other called *Pekhery*, "He who surrounds."

The hieroglyphs read from right to left, the inscription therefore begins on the right-hand side. "(1) He [who] is on this door, he opens unto Ra. Sa [says] unto Pekhery, Open thy gate unto Ra, unbolt thy door for the Horizon-god. It is that he makes light the thick darkness. (2) The gate it is of entrance (?) before the souls who are in *Amentet*, after entering this gate. (3) He [who] is on this gate, he opens unto Ra. Sa [says] to Pekhery, Open thy gate to Ra, unbolt thy door to the Horizon-god. He is accustomed to make light the thick darkness. (4)

The Gate it is of entrance before the souls who are in *Amentet* after entering this gate of *Amentet*. He rises behind this great god.

The long line of inscription at the extreme right of the page begins the next scene: "This great god arrives at this pylon. The gods, who are in it, worship him."

Then comes the picture of a structure which has given the name of "Book of Gates" to this portion of the religious literature of Egypt. The Duat was divided into twelve parts, corresponding with the twelve hours of the night; at the end of each hour was a gate through which the sun passed in his nightly journey through the Duat. The gate itself was a narrow passage between high walls, on the tops of which was the *kheker*-ornament forming a sort of *chevaux-de-frise*. The name of this gate, which is partly obliterated, can be restored as *Zesert-bau*, "Sacred of souls," from the sarcophagus of Sety I. A human guardian stands at the entrance and the exit, the one at the top holds a knife and is called Bay; the rest of the hieroglyphs read, "He stretches out his two hands unto Ra, kindling a spark for Ra." At the angles are two serpents, from whose mouths flow a continuous stream of poison. Beside the gate are two tall poles surmounted by human heads; these are respectively Khepera and Atum, the morning sun and evening sun; their names being inscribed above their heads. The line of hieroglyphs between them reads: "They stand upon their heads. They are upon their long poles, standing upon them at the gate in the earth."

20. PL. XIV. This scene shows the eleventh division of the Duat or Other World. It occurs in other places, but perhaps one of the best representations is on the sarcophagus of Sety I. The scene is divided, as is usual, into three registers; the middle one (B) representing the way of the solar boat, which is preceded by various divinities, the upper (A) and lower (C) registers represent the banks of the river on which the boat floats.

A. A crocodile-headed god leads the way; he holds an *uas*-sceptre in his right hand, and in his left, which is behind his back, is a serpent with its head erect. His name is Sebek-er, or, according to M. Lefébure (*Rec. of Past*, xii, 11), Sebek-Ra. Eight women seated on coiled serpents, one hand resting on the serpent's head, the other holding a star. These are the stars of dawn, and are called "All the stars which are in Nut."

Three hawk-headed figures standing. Their names are Sopd, an almost obliterated word, which reads Shenebt on the sarcophagus of Sety, and He who is in the Double Boat. Four ram-headed figures standing, called respectively, Khnum, Peneter, Dend, and Ba. The inscription is the same as that on the sarcophagus of Sety, which has been translated by M. Lefébure (*Rec. of Past*, xii, 12).

" . . . . . not arrives Ra. Those who are in this scene, their sceptres are in their hands, it is they who make firm the shrine, their two arms being at the side of the body which is in the Double Boat of the god, after issuing from the gate of the land of Sma. They place the oars in heaven [when] the hour which is in front [i.e. the future] comes into being . . . . Those who are in this scene, their serpents being under them, their hands holding stars, they issue from the double sanctuary of this great god, two to the east and two to the west. It is they who worship their souls of the east. They offer praises to this god, they worship him after his going forth, and Sedeti [when] he issues in his shapes. It is they who lead this god, they adore this god, they   . to them, their serpents rising upwards behind him in this scene. He advances at their advance, they take their station before this god. They turn round the gods at this gate . . . . . . of *Amentet*." The meaning of the concluding sentence is not clear; I have therefore not translated it.

B. A god standing, holding an *uas*-sceptre in one hand and an *ankh* in the other. His name is *Sebekhui*, "He of the Pylon." Two women standing, wearing the crowns of Upper and Lower Egypt. Their names are not at all clear in meaning, and the sarcophagus of Sety gives no help.

Four monkeys, each holding a gigantic hand, *Mesu uaut*, "The children of the roads." Then comes a snake chained to the earth with four chains fastened with hooks shaped like the hieroglyph for S. This is Apep, the serpent of evil, the enemy of Osiris and the gods. *Advancing towards him are eight figures, four jackal-headed and four human-headed, each carrying a knife and a hook of the shape like the hooks which fasten Apep.* The inscription reads: " . . . the children when they strike him, they rest in Nut. Those who are in this scene, they spread out his chains. It is that his teeth are in heaven,

---

* All figures which occur between asterisks * are put in from notes, the inscriptions on this plate are also from a hand copy and are not in fac-simile.

and his poison goes down to *Amentet.* Those who are in this scene, it is they who establish Ra in the eastern horizon of heaven. They direct this god, their staves (?) in (?) their hands, two to the left and two to the right, in the two sanctuaries of this god. They go forth behind him, praising his soul [when] they see it. It is they who make firm his disk. Those who are in this scene, they turn themselves towards this pylon of Duaty [Him of the Duat], opening the çaverns and making firm their secret pylons. The souls, they arise behind him."

C. A cat-headed god holding an *uas*-sceptre in his right hand; in his left, which is behind his back, is a lotus. On the sarcophagus of Sety the god holds a serpent. The name is *Mauty*, " He of the cat." Four men bowing, called *Auïtyu.* *Four women standing, [*Ke*]*byut*, " The mourners." Four women wearing the crown of Lower Egypt, and four wearing the crown of Upper Egypt.*

The inscription reads: " . . . . behind him, their bodies are in their place. Those who are in this scene, naming Ra ; great are the names of his transformations. Their souls, they ascend behind him, when their bodies remain in their place. Those who are in this scene raise up truth and make it firm in the shrine of Ra when he sets in Nut. Their souls, they ascend behind him, their bodies remain in their place. Those who are in this scene, it is they who fix the duration of time, and make the years to come into existence for the guardians of the desolate ones in the Duat and for the Living Ones in heaven, namely, they who follow this god. Those who are in this scene in this pylon, they are uncovered as to their hair before this great god in *Amentet.* They turn themselves towards this pylon, entering not into heaven. Those who are in this scene they worship Ra, they offer praises to him, they adore him when they worship the gods who are in the Duat and the gatekeepers of the secret places. They remain in their place. The doorkeeper of the cavern (*Qerert*) remains in his place."

21. PL. XV. The sunrise is shown on the east wall of the north passage. It had been painted in red and black, but is now greatly faded, and in places the figures and hieroglyphs are barely visible. I think that it is still unfinished, and that the painting was merely a temporary decoration put up until it was possible to sculpture the scenes in the same way as on the opposite wall. Otherwise

I cannot account for the first draft of the inscription being still visible here and there, as is shown by the signs in dotted lines, which were as distinct as the other hieroglyphs. Only two colours, red and black, were used here, whereas four colours, red, black, white, and blue, were used on the sculptured walls. It seems probable then that this East wall shows us merely the artist's sketch, which was never finished.

The scene has the pathway of the sun, as in the sunset, with the solar disk in the middle. From the disk issue Horus the Child, emblematic of the youthful Sun, and the ram-headed Beetle, emblematic of creation and resurrection. Two pathways diverge from the disk diagonally across the scene, defining the limits of the celestial river. Above the upper diagonal path are seven bowing figures, turned upside down. They are called, *Sheta Kheperu*, "Secret of transformations ; " *Sheta yru*, "Secret of forms ; " *Az* (?) *mesut*, " . . . . . of births ; " *Ymy ta*, " He who is in the earth ; " *Khenti-ta*, " Chief of the earth ; " *Meny*, " He who establishes ; " *Khesny.* Between them and the sun's path are three lines of hieroglyphs: " These gods who are in this scene, they give praise (?) to Ra . . . . companion (?) when he enters (?) from the womb of Nut."

Between the diverging paths are eight lines of hieroglyphs: (1) " We draw Ra, we follow this only lord, (2) Khepera, chief lord. Hail to thee, the great one, (3) ye are glorious. Living soul of my transformations. (4) Peace, peace, within his disk. Ra rests within (5) his disk. This great god enters into his eastern hill, chief of the (6) gods, seeing the past generations (*pat*), shining on the present generations (*rekhyt*) (7) blessed is the face of him upon earth by these gods." The last line is too obscure to translate.

CHAPTER IV.

THE SMALL OBJECTS.

22. A few small objects were found in the filling of the passages and halls, apparently having been thrown away as mere rubbish. The building itself had evidently been rifled, and every object removed, whether of value or not.

PL. XVII, 3. A tall pottery stand of a form characteristic of the XIXth Dynasty.

4 and 5. SCULPTOR'S TRIAL PIECES.—There seems to have been a school of sculpture in the Temple of Rameses, for on the plain surface of the walls below the decoration in that temple are sketches of figures roughly incised. These trial pieces probably belonged to the same school. The first exercise of the youthful sculptor was invariably the *neb* sign, giving, as it did, a straight line, and a semi-circular curve. It is interesting to see the sign engraved by the master's hand at the top of the stone, below are the student's attempts in every degree of badness. Another piece which was found showed part of a little scene of the worship of Osiris; it was unfinished, one figure only having been sculptured, the rest being merely sketched in in black. This piece is now at South Kensington. The two pieces shown in this plate must have been done by advanced students. No. 4 is the more interesting, as it is not completely finished, the original drawing in black ink is still visible at the shoulder. The serpent seems to have been added so as to fill up the blank space and not waste the stone.

6. PLASTER CASTS.—These are casts of the eyes of statues and of details of decoration; which, as the cartouche shows, were probably from the temple of Rameses. They must therefore belong to the same school of sculpture as the trial-pieces, and served the same purpose as the plaster casts in schools of art at the present day.

7. A SURVEYOR'S MARK.—This is of the Roman period.

All these objects were found at the North end, and in the North passage.

23. In the Hall and South Chamber were found the Coptic ostrakon (PL. XXXVII, p. 43), and a small squatting statuette (PL. XIX) of limestone. The statuette was without a head, and was inscribed both back and front. From the style and workmanship it belongs to the XXVIth Dynasty.

In front is a representation of ·Osiris standing on a pedestal in a boat, and holding the *heq* sign, emblem of sovereignty in his hands. The inscriptions on each side are so corrupt as to be almost unreadable. That in front of the figure appears to be merely the name and titles of the god: "Speech of Osiris, the great god, ruler (?) of eternity." The inscription behind the figure: "Speech of the lord (?) of Deddu. [May he] give funeral offerings which the gods love."

Down the back of the statuette are five rows of hieroglyphs, the top part being slightly broken away. (1) "May the king give an offering unto Osiris-Khenti-Amentiu, the great god, Lord of [Abydos]; (2) may he give funeral offerings of bread and beer, oxen and fowls, incense (?) and ointment, wine and milk; that which heaven gives, which earth produces, and which the Nile brings (3) from his cavern, and on which the god lives, for the *ka* of the divine father, the *heu-ka* priest of the mysteries of the book of eternity in his month, (4) of the second class and of the fourth class of priests; of the first class and second class of priests in the place of decrees, the *uab*-priest of the Boat of the second class, Hor-se (5) . . . . . . son of one of the same rank, Hor-nekht, true of voice, son of one of the same rank, Hor-se-ast, true of voice."

The inscription round the base gives the same name and title as before: ". . . of the same rank, Hor-nekht." Another fragment shows that the mother's name was given, but nothing remains of the name.

24. Hieratic ostraka. A few limestone ostraka, inscribed in hieratic, were found. Of nine of these Mr. Griffith has kindly given the following translations and notes:—

1. "Sunre, son of Shesuaf (?), his mother being Yua, of Pa-shes (?)" "Amu-nefer, son of Rui, his mother being Huta, of Pa-shes (?)" A memorandum of the two people named.

2. "How hast thou forgotten the business that I told thee!" The text is complete, perhaps only a trial of the pen.

3. "220 nails (?) worth 9 kite."

4. Possibly a bargain of some sort concerning sandals. The first word appears not to be *sunt*.

6. The ape of Thoth seated on a base, a lotus flower (?) before him, and an obscure inscription behind.

7. A list of names, Sun-re, Pen-dua, Sety, Amenemapt, and amounts, 14, &c.

8. A list of words or names and numbers.

9. Memoranda, with others added, after the stone had been turned upside down.

25. Demotic ostraka. A very few demotic ostraka were found, chiefly on potsherds. Professor Spiegelberg kindly read them, and says that they are all accounts, (1) oil, (3) wine, (4) salt, (5) gives measures, but no material is mentioned.

CHAPTER V.

THE WORSHIP OF OSIRIS.

26. *Legend of Osiris.*—From the Greek authors we are able to get a fairly connected account of Osiris. They agree that he came from the north, Plutarch saying that he was born on the right side of the world, which he explains as the north; but Diodorus mentions the town from which he came, namely, Nysa in Arabia Felix, on the borders of Egypt. The Book of the Dead gives his birth-place as Deddu (Busiris), and this statement is given by Plutarch on the authority of Eudoxus. Plutarch gives the legend of his birth on the first of the intercalary days (see Nut, sect. 13, No. 13) as the firstborn of the deities Geb and Nut, and says that on his entrance into the world a voice was heard saying, "The Lord of all the earth is born," but Diodorus speaks of him as a human king. The two Greek authors, Plutarch and Diodorus, go on to tell us that on coming to the throne Osiris proceeded to teach his subjects the arts of civilization, introducing corn and the vine, and reclaiming the Egyptians from cannibalism and barbarism. Having reduced his own kingdom to civilization and order, he gave the government into the hands of his wife Isis, and travelled southwards up the Nile, teaching the people as he went. The army that accompanied him was divided into companies, to each of whom he gave a standard. He was accompanied also by musicians and dancers, and he introduced the art of music, as well as the knowledge of agriculture into all the countries through which he passed. He built Thebes of the hundred Gates, and at Aswan he made a dam to regulate the inundation of the Nile. He travelled through the then known world, which included India and Asia Minor, and ended his peaceful mission by returning happily and in triumph to Egypt. There he found everything in order, but his brother Set, consumed with jealousy and longing to usurp the kingdom, determined on his death. To this end, Set, with his fellow-conspirators, invited Osiris, under pretence of friendship, to a banquet, and there exhibited a wooden coffer, beautifully decorated, which he promised to give to any one whose body it fitted. All the conspirators in turn lay down in it, but it fitted none of them, for the measurements had been carefully taken from Osiris himself without his knowledge. Osiris un-suspectingly entered the coffer and lay down, where-upon Set and his companions hastily clapped on the cover, nailed it down, and poured molten lead over it. They then carried the coffer down to the Nile and threw it into the water. Here there comes a discrepancy in the narrative. According to the Metternich stele, one of the few Egyptian authorities extant, Isis fled to Buto, in the marshes of the Delta, to escape from Set, and there she brought forth her son Horus, and remained in that place till he was old enough to do battle with his father's murderer. Plutarch, however, makes no mention of this, but says that Isis was at Koptos when she heard of the death of Osiris, that she cut off a lock of her hair and put on mourning apparel, and at once instituted a search for her husband's body. After many wanderings she arrived at Byblos, and found that the coffer had lodged in the branches of a tamarisk tree. The tree had grown round it and had become so large and luxuriant as to attract the notice and admiration of the king of Byblos, who had it cut down and made it into a pillar to support the roof of his palace. Isis became nurse to the infant prince and in reward for her services was permitted to open the pillar and remove the coffer. She took it away into the desert and there opened it, and throwing herself on the corpse wept and lamented. Afterwards she hid away the chest with the body still inside it, and went to Buto, where her son Horus resided, pre-sumably meaning to return and bury the dead Osiris. Meanwhile, however, Set, hunting wild boars by moonlight, came across the coffer and recognized it. In his fury he flung it open, tore the body to pieces, and scattered the fragments far and wide. Isis, on her return, found what had occurred. Mourning and lamenting she searched through the length and breadth of Egypt, burying each piece of the body in the place where she found it, and raising to its memory a temple or a shrine.

This is the legend of Osiris as it was known in Greek times. From what Herodotus says, and from other indications in mythological texts, it would seem that the Egyptians, like the Jews and Hindus, had a Supreme Deity whose name it was not lawful to mention, and who manifested himself, as in Hinduism, under many forms and names. It appears evident that this Supreme God was known commonly among the Egyptians by the name of Osiris, but his true name was hidden from all except those initiated into the mysteries. In the pyramid texts, Unas says, "O great god, whose name is unknown." On the stele of Re-ma there is the same expression, "His name is not known."

E

An observation of Herodotus proves that Osiris was the chief deity, in Greek times at least, for he says that though the Egyptians were not agreed upon the worship of their different gods they were united in the cult of Osiris.

It is this confusion of names and forms that makes the study of Osiris so difficult, and I have endeavoured to point out only a few of his many manifestations.

27. *Osiris as a Sun-god.*—Egyptologists have generally looked upon Osiris as a form of the Sun-god, and, indeed, it is usually said that Ra is the living or day-sun and Osiris the dead or night-sun. This view, however, is not altogether borne out by the mythology of the Egyptians themselves, except in so far as that almost every deity of any note was, at some period of his career, identified with the sun by the worshippers of Ra. Even in the Book of Am Duat and the Book of Gates, which are entirely concerned with the journey of the sun during the hours of the night, it is Ra who passes by in his boat, whose devoted followers gather round to protect him from danger, to whom the gates, which divide the hours, are flung open. Osiris, on the contrary, is not the hero of this nocturnal journey. In the Book of Gates he appears only once, and then at the entrance of the Sun into the Duat or other world. There he is seen (PL. XIII.) encircling the Duat and supporting Nut, who receives Ra in her arms. It is quite evident here that Osiris and the sun are two distinct personalities. In chap. xvii of the Book of the Dead Ra is identified with Osiris, but the original text and the glosses are so obscure that it is not possible to make out the true meaning. In the hymn to Ra, which comes between chaps. xv and xvi, there is a very definite statement about the night sun, showing that it is Ra himself and not Osiris. "Thou (Ra) completest the hours of the Night, according as thou hast measured them out. And when thou hast completed them according to thy rule, day dawneth." All through the Book of the Dead, though it is implied that Osiris and Ra are the same, yet there is no definite statement of the fact. M. Jequier thinks that the whole of the Book of Am Duat, and particularly the Book of Gates, is an attempt of the theologians of the XVIIIth and XIXth Dynasties to reconcile the solar with the Osirian worship.

28. *Osiris as the Moon-god.*—Osiris is identified with the moon quite as readily as with the sun. Chap. lxv of the Book of the Dead gives prayers to the moon couched in precisely the same terms as the petitions to Osiris. "O thou who shinest forth from the Moon, thou who givest light from the Moon, let me come forth at large amid thy train . . . . let the Duat be opened for me . . . let me come forth upon this day." In the Lamentations of Isis and Nephthys, Osiris is actually identified with the moon. "Thoth . . . . placeth thy soul in the barque Maat, in that name which is thine of God Moon . . . . Thou comest to us as a child each month" (DE HORRACK, *Rec. of Past*, ii). Again, in the Book of the Dead, chap. viii, "I am the same Osiris, the dweller in Amentet. . . . . I am the Moon-god who dwelleth among the gods." Plutarch says that upon the new moon of Phamenoth, which falls in the beginning of spring, a festival was celebrated which was called The entrance of Osiris into the Moon.

Another proof of the connection of Osiris with the moon is that the lunar festivals of the Month and the Half-month, i.e. the New Moon and the Full Moon, are specially dedicated to him from very early times; he is also Lord of the Sixth-day festival (the first quarter of the moon), and the Tenait (the last quarter) is one of his sacred days, and one specially observed at Abydos.

The two ceremonies recorded by Plutarch may also have a connection with the worship of Osiris Lunus, as the principal object was made in the form of a crescent. At the funeral of Osiris, a tree was cut down and the trunk formed into the shape of a crescent. The other ceremony was more elaborate. "On the 19th of Pachons they march in procession to the sea-side, whither likewise the priests and other proper officers carry the sacred chest, wherein is enclosed a small boat or vessel of gold. Into this they first pour some fresh water, and then all that are present cry out with a loud voice, 'Osiris is found.' As soon as this ceremony is finished, they throw a little fresh mould, together with some rich odours and spices, into this water, mixing the whole mass together and working it up into a little image in the shape of a crescent, which image they afterwards dress up and adorn with a proper habit."

Herodotus says that "pigs were sacrificed to Bacchus, and to the moon when completely full. When they offer this sacrifice to the moon, and have killed the victim, they put the end of his tail, with the spleen and the fat, into a caul found in the body of the animal, all of which they burn on the sacred fire, and eat the rest of the flesh on the day of the full moon. Those who, on account of their poverty, cannot bear the expense of this sacrifice, mould a paste into the form of a hog and make their offering. In the evening of the festival of Bacchus, though everyone be obliged to kill a swine before the door of his house, yet he immediately restores the carcase to the hog-herd that sold it to him. The rest of this festival is celebrated in Egypt to the honour of Bacchus with the same ceremonies as in Greece." The Grecian ceremonies being phallic, it is evident that Osiris Lunus was the same deity as Osiris Generator, and it is this idea that Hermes Trismegistos expresses when he calls the moon the instrument of birth. Though we only hear of the sacrifice of pigs to Osiris and the moon in Greek times, yet we have an evident allusion to it as early as the XIXth Dynasty. On the sarcophagus of Sety I, and in the tomb of Rameses V, there are representations of Osiris enthroned, and before him is a boat in which stands a pig being beaten by an ape. The ape is the emblem of Thoth, who is one of the chief lunar deities. So in this scene we have the combination of Osiris and the moon in connection with the pig.

Bronze figures of Osiris-Lunus are not uncommon. In this form he is never represented as a mummy, but wears the short kilt, and on his head the disk of the moon, and sometimes the horns of the crescent. The Sacred Eye is either in his hand or engraved on the disk, and his name, Osiris-Aah, is on the pedestal.

29. *Osiris as a god of vegetation.* One of the principal forms under which Osiris is worshipped is as a god of vegetation and generation. Hymns addressed to him are full of allusions to his generative power. "Nothing is made living without him, the Lord of Life" (*Stele of Re-ma*). "Through thee the world waxeth green in triumph before the might of Neb-er-Zer" (*Pap. of Ani*).

And, in a hymn of the time of Rameses IX, Osiris is worshipped as the god from whom all life comes :—
" Thou art praised, thou who stretchest out thine arms, who sleepest on thy side, who liest on the sand, the Lord of the ground, thou mummy with the long phallus. . . . . . The earth lies on thine arm and its corners upon thee from here to the four supports of heaven. Shouldst thou move, then trembles the earth. . . . . . [The Nile] comes forth from the

sweat of thy hands. Thou spuest out the air that is in thy throat into the nostrils of mankind. Divine is that on which one lives. It . . . . . in thy nostrils, the tree and its leafage, the reeds and the . . ., barley, wheat, and fruit trees. . . . . . . Thou art the father and mother of mankind, they live on thy breath, they subsist on the flesh of thy body " (ERMAN, *A Z.*, 1900, 30-33). Mr. Fraser (*Golden Bough*, i, 304) suggests that the Dad-pillar, the well-known emblem often called the Backbone of Osiris, "might very well be a conventional representation of a tree stripped of its leaves, and, if Osiris was a tree-spirit, the bare trunk and branches of a tree might naturally be described as his backbone."

Osiris, as the begetter of mankind, is identified with the god Min of Koptos, the god of generation, and the Phallic festivals celebrated in honour of Osiris are said by Plutarch to be precisely the same as those in honour of Bacchus, the similarity of worship being so great that the two Greek authors who have left us the most detailed account of the Egyptian religion do not hesitate to speak of Osiris as Bacchus.

The ritual of the worship of Osiris as a god of vegetation is preserved in a Ptolemaic inscription at Dendereh. There we have the exact details of the celebration of the Ploughing Festival to which allusions are made in texts relating to Osiris. The ritual of Abydos is followed by Koptos, Elephantine, Kusae, Diospolis of Lower Egypt, Hermopolis, Athribis, and Schedia ; but in Busiris, Heracleopolis Magna, Sais, and Netert it differed in several particulars. To take Abydos first, as the chief place of worship in Upper Egypt, the ceremony was performed in the presence of the cow-goddess Shenty. In the temple of Sety at Abydos there is a coloured bas-relief of the goddess in the inner chamber at the back, and it is probable that this chamber is the Per-Shenty (House or Chamber of Shenty) where some of the mysteries of the death and resurrection of Osiris were celebrated. A hollow statuette of pure gold was made in the likeness of the god—that is to say, of a man bandaged like a mummy—with the high crown of Upper Egypt. It was to be a cubit long, including the crown, and two palms wide. Then the reliquary was of black copper, and its length two palms and three fingers, its breadth three palms and three fingers, and its height one palm. On the twelfth of Khoiak four *hin* of sand and one *hin* of barley were put into the statuette, which was then laid in the "garden" with rushes over and under it.

The " garden " was in the Per-Shenty, and was made of stone, four-square and resting on four pillars. It was a cubit and two palms in length and breadth, and three palms three fingers deep inside. The statuette was wrapped in a *shet*-garment and decorated with a necklace and a blue flower laid beside it. On the 21st of Khoiak, nine days after, all the sand and barley was taken out of the statuette, and dry incense put in its place. The statuette was then bandaged with four strips of fine linen, and was laid daily in the sun until the " day of resting in the chamber of Sokar." On the 25th of Khoiak the statuette which had been made the previous year was brought out and laid on a bier, and was buried the same day in the burial-place called the Arq-heh. This Arq-heh was probably a small shrine ; as Pef-tot-nit (Louvre, A 93), in describing what he had done for the temple of Osiris at Abydos, says, " The Arq-heh was of a single block of syenite." There was, besides, another mystic ceremony, the making of what Brugsch, in his translation, calls, " Kü-gelchen," but which should more properly be called cylinders. This mystical ceremony was, apparently, not performed at Abydos. The cylinders were to be made of barley, date-meal, dried balsam, fresh resin, fourteen kinds of sweet-smelling spices, and fourteen kinds of precious stones (according to the number of the relics of the god) mixed together with water from the holy lake, and made in the form of little balls, which were wrapped in sycomore leaves.

At Busiris the ritual was rather different, as might be expected from the different character of the god. The festival did not begin till the 20th of Khoiak, when the barley and sand were put into the " gardens " in the Per-Shenty. Then fresh inundation water was poured out of a golden vase over both the goddess and the "garden," and the barley was allowed to grow as the emblem of the resurrection of the god after his burial in the earth, " for the growth of the garden is the growth of the divine substance." The later date is owing to the later harvest of the north. At Philae there is a representation of the god lying on his bier, a priest pouring water over him, and plants growing out of his body (*M.A.F.*, tome xiii, pl. 40). On the sarcophagus of Ankhrui found at Hawara there is a similar picture (PETRIE, *Hawara*, pl. ii). In the Museum at Marseilles there is a basalt sarcophagus of the Saite period, on which is en-graved a scene described thus by M. Maspero : " A hillock, rounded at the top and crowned with four cone-shaped trees ; the inscription tells us that it is

Osiris who rests here." This is the same scene as those already cited, of plants growing from the body of Osiris, though here the grave only, and not the body, are shown.

Representations of the resurrection of Osiris are seen at Dendereh, more literally and not so poeti-cally expressed as at Philae. At Dendereh the god leaps alive from his bier with the mummy wrap-pings still upon him (MAR. *Dendereh* iv, pls. 72, 90). The little cylinders were to be finished on the 14th, and placed inside the statuette on the 16th. The linen in which the statuette was wrapped had to be made in one day, and the wrapping took place on the 24th. But the 30th of Khoiak was the great day at Busiris, for then was performed the great ceremony of the Uplifting of the Dad-pillar. The statuette was buried in a grave called (by Brugsch) " The Depth above Earth." The Dad-pillar was to remain standing for ten days. This raising of the Dad is a very curious ceremony, but no satisfactory explanation of it has yet been made. One of the best-known representations of it is at Abydos in the Hall of the Osirian mysteries, where Isis and the king, Sety I, are raising the pillar between them, and there is also a picture of the Dad firmly set up and swathed with cloth. Still earlier is a scene in the tomb of Kheru-ef at Assassif, copied by Prof. Erman, where Amenhotep III, attended by his queen and the royal daughters, is setting up the Dad-pillar " on the morning of the Sed-festivals," while the sacred cattle "go round the walls four times " (BRUGSCH, *Thes.*, 1190).

As the god of vegetation certain trees and plants must of necessity be under his special protection ; and this we find to be the case. To him were sacred the tamarisk and the sont-acacia ; and at Busiris the necropolis, in which his effigy was annually buried, was called Aat-en-beh, Place of Palm-branches. Amt, the Town of the Acacia-trees, was so completely identified with him in his bull form that it was called Apis by the Greeks. Diodorus remarks that the ivy was sacred to Osiris as to Bacchus, and Plutarch says that a fig-leaf was the emblem of the god, and that his votaries were forbidden to cut down any fruit-trees or to mar any springs of water.

The ritual of Dendereh continued in practice until Roman times, for figures of Osiris made of barley and sand were found by Drs. Grenfell and Hunt at Sheikh Fadl, the ancient Kynopolis. These figures were roughly modelled to the desired shape, and were then bandaged after the fashion of a mummy with patches of gilding here and there, to represent the golden statuette enjoined by the priests of Dendereh. The little cylinders, which contained sand and barley, but no precious stones, were found with the figures. The coffin which contained the figure has the hawk head of Horus, and across the breast is the winged scarab, emblem of the resurrection. Some were found in a little chamber built of stones, which seems to correspond with the Arq-heh of Abydos. Two dedicatory tablets were with the figures, on one of which was the date of the twelfth year of Trajan. This shows that the ceremony did not die out till the introduction of Christianity. The ritual was certainly of much earlier date than the inscription of Dendereh, and a modification of the ceremony was used in the XVIIIth Dynasty at the burial of a king. In Ma-her-pra's tomb at Thebes "there was found a symbolic bier with a mattress, &c., and on the top a figure of Osiris painted on linen. Earth had been placed on this figure and grains of corn sown and watered there so that they sprouted " (*Arch. Rep. of the E.E.F.*, 1898-99, p. 25).

30. *Osiris as god of the Nile.* As the creator of all things living, Osiris is also god of the Nile, for it is to the river that Egypt owes her fertility. Plutarch, who as a careful folk-lorist noted all details of ritual, observes that the Greeks allegorise Saturn into Time and Juno into Air, and in the same way by Osiris the Egyptians mean the Nile. But he goes on to say that there are other philosophers who think that by Osiris is not meant the Nile only but the principle and power of moisture in general, looking upon this as the cause of generation and what gives being to the seminal substance. They imagine, he continues, that Osiris is of a black colour because water gives a black cast to everything with which it is mixed. This gives a very curious derivation for the name Kem-ur, The great black One, under which name Osiris is mentioned several times in the Book of the Dead. " I flood the land with water, and Kem-ur is my name " (chap. lxiv). When he is set as Judge of the Dead, his throne stands upon water, out of which grows the lotus that supports the four Children of Horus. Offerings almost invariably include the lotus, the most striking of the water-plants of Egypt. In the Sed-festival of Osorkon II, the Osirified king, wearing the white crown, stands with a stream of water pouring from his hands. This is evidently the scene to which the hymn already quoted (sect. 29) refers, " The Nile comes forth from

the sweat of thy hands." The king as Osiris personifies the Nile, and wears the crown of Upper Egypt as the country from which the Nile comes.

31. *Osiris as god and judge of the Dead.*—It is in this capacity that Osiris is best known, for everyone is familiar with the scene of the Weighing of the Heart, where the deceased are weighed in the scales against each other. Anubis watches the pointer of the balance, Maat or the ape of Thoth sits on the upright support, Thoth enters the record on his tablet ; the deceased recites the Negative Confession, and watches the proceedings anxiously, for near the balance crouches the horrible animal, Amemt, the Eater of Hearts, ready to devour any heart which fails to balance the feather exactly. At a little distance the impartial judge, Osiris, sits enthroned, surrounded by all the splendour that the artist could contrive. Sometimes another scene is shown, where the deceased, after passing the ordeal of the Scales in safety, is led by Thoth to the foot of the throne and there presented to Osiris. The speech of Thoth and the prayer of the deceased are given, but the reply of Osiris is never found.

As god of the dead, there are several points of great interest. According to the inscription, Horus buried his father with great pomp, and all the funeral ceremonies in Egypt were supposed to be an exact imitation of those used for the burial of Osiris. The paintings and sculptures in the tombs of the kings are distinctly said to be a copy of those with which Horus decorated the tomb of his father. It is therefore evident that in the funeral ceremonies used at the entombment of a king or a high official we shall find some at least of the ritual of the worship of Osiris as god of the dead.

32. *Sacrifices.* One custom which was never omitted at a great funeral was the sacrificing, and this brings us to one of the most interesting points of the ritual. That it was to Osiris that the sacrifices were made is shown by a passage in the Book of the Dead, " Oh Terrible One, who art over the Two Lands, Red God who orderest the block of execution, to whom is given the Double [Urert] Crown and Enjoyment as Prince of Henen-seten " (chap. xvii). The dead being identified with Osiris would require sacrifices as gods, and the scene of the slaughter and dismemberment of cattle is very common in tombs and temples. The question now arises as to whether animals were merely substitutes for human victims. Porphyry says that, according to Manetho, Amasis abolished human sacrifice at Heliopolis. Diodorus reports that in ancient times the kings sacrificed red-haired men at the sepulchre of Osiris, by which may be meant either the traditional sepulchre of the god, or more probably the tomb of a predecessor of the royal sacrificer. Plutarch is even more explicit ; he quotes Manetho to the effect that in the city of Eilitheiya it was the custom to sacrifice men annually and in public, by burning them alive, their ashes being afterwards scattered. The human victim was called Typho. Turning to the evidence of the monuments, we find in the temple of Dendereh a human figure with a hare's head, tied to a stake before Osiris Khenti-Amentiu (Mar. *Dend.* iv, pl. lvi), and Horus is shown in a Ptolemaic sculpture at Karnak killing a bound hare-headed figure before the bier of Osiris, who is re-presented in the form of Harpocrates. That these figures are really human beings with the head of an animal fastened on is proved by another sculpture at Dendereh (*id. ib.* pl. lxxxi), where a kneeling man has the hawk's head and wings over his head and shoulders, and in another place, a priest has the jackal's head on his shoulders, his own head appearing through the disguise (*id. ib.* pl. xxxi). Besides, Diodorus tells us that the Egyptian kings in former times had worn on their heads the fore-part of a lion, or of a bull, or of a dragon, showing that this method of disguise or transformation was a well-known custom.

In the Book of the Dead, sacrifices of human beings, or of animals in the place of human victims, are alluded to frequently, sometimes in set terms. " The Great Circle of gods at the Great Hoeing in Deddu, when the associates of Set arrive and take the form of goats, slay them in the presence of the gods there, while their blood runneth down " (chap. xviii). " Horus cutteth off their heads in heaven when in the forms of winged fowl, their hinder parts on earth when in the forms of quadrupeds or in water as fishes. All fiends, male or female, the Osiris N. destroyeth them " (chap. cxxxiv). " I have come, and I have slain for thee him that attacked thee. I have come, and I have brought unto thee the fiends of Set with their fetters upon them. I have come, and I have made sacrificial victims of those who were hostile to thee. I have come, and I have made sacrifices unto thee of thine animals and victims for slaughter " (chap. clxxiii).

Plutarch, when describing the animals reserved for sacrifice, observes that no bullock may be offered to the gods which has not the seal of the priests first stamped upon it. He then quotes Castor to the effect that this seal has on it the impress of a man kneeling with his hands tied behind him and a sword pointed at his throat.

When we remember what Plutarch says also about the human victim being called Set, and that according to Diodorus the victim was red-haired, red being the colour of Set, it is evident that in the sacrificial animals we have the substitutes for the human victim, and we may expect to find at the funerals of kings and great officials that the human sacrifice is continued to a comparatively late date.

In the sculptures of the XVIIIth Dynasty tombs of Sennefer, Paheri, Rekh-ma-Ra, Renni, and Mentu-her-khepesh-ef, a human figure is depicted which has been recognized by M. Lefébure and others as the sacrificial victim. He is called the *Teknu*, and in the tombs of Rekh-ma-Ra and Sennefer he is wrapped in an ox-skin with only his head visible. In the other tombs the *Teknu* crouches down on the sledge on which he is being drawn to the place of sacrifice. In the sculptures of Mentu-her-khepesh-ef, it appears that the ritual enforced the strangling of the victim and the destruction of the body by fire, which supports Plutarch's statement of the human sacrifice by fire.

In the tomb of Kenni (pl. xii) at El Kab, the victim, here called Kenu, is kneeling upright on a small sledge, so swathed in cloth that only the outline of the figure is visible. The sledge is drawn by several men, and the inscription reads " Bringing the Kenu to this Underworld."

The ebony tablets of Mena (Petrie, *Royal Tombs* ii, pl. iii, 2, 4, 6) give a sacrificial scene, in which the victim is a human being. Tablet No. 2 gives a bound captive kneeling before the *ka*-name of the king ; this is probably the first scene of the sacrificial ceremony of which we get the principal scene in the other tablets. No. 6 shows a kneeling captive whose arms are bound behind him ; before him sits a man who strikes him to the heart with a small weapon. Behind the sacrificial priest is a standing figure holding a staff ; and behind the victim are a long pole, and the hide of an animal, which is in later times the symbol of Ami-Ut, a god of the dead. Above the scene is the hieroglyph Shesep. No. 4, though greatly broken, gives many details which have been destroyed in No. 6. The sacrifice has completely disappeared, only the head of the standing figure remains. Behind him, however, is the sign for a palace or fortress, and behind that is the *ka*-name, *Aha*, of King Mena. We can also see that the long pole behind the victim is one of the sacred standards surmounted by a hawk. The sign *Mes* (Born of, or Child) is above the hawk, and the sign Shesep occurs again with the hieroglyphs for South and· North above it. It is evident that Shesep, which means "to receive," has here some special technical meaning.

There is also the legend, given by Herodotus, of Hercules being led before Jupiter to be sacrificed. Herodotus treats the legend with scorn, the custom being so totally at variance with the mild and gentle character of the Egyptians of his day. But the truth of the story is at once apparent when taken in connection with other instances of human sacrifices. The name Busiris, which Diodorus mentions as a fabulous king who sacrificed his guests, points to the place where the victims were immolated ; and seeing that the raising of the Dad-pillar was the chief religious event of the year, it was probably before that object of worship that the sacrifices were performed.

In the tomb of Amenhotep II, three human bodies were found, but though there is no actual proof that these were the victims of sacrifice yet from their position it seems likely that they had been immolated in honour of the dead king.

33. In considering Osiris as god of the dead, it is necessary to remember that every dead person in later times was identified with him and was called by his name. In the early dynasties this was not the custom, only kings being honoured in this manner. Men-kau-Ra is the first of whom we have any record who bears the name of Osiris, though we shall see further on (Osiris in the Sed-festival) that the king in his life-time was identified with the god. In the XIIth Dynasty the custom became general, and in the XVIIIth it was universal, every dead person being called Osiris. The complete identification of the king with Osiris is shown in a sculpture in the tomb of Horemheb (L. D. iii, 78, A and B), where Thothmes III is enthroned as Osiris in a shrine, before him are four human figures called respectively Amset, Hapi, Duamutef, and Qebhsennuf, with the cartouches of Neb-maat-Ra, Men-kheperu-Ra, Aa-kheperu-Ra, and Menkheper-Ra. The Weighing of the Heart takes place in the presence of these royal personages in exactly the same manner as though they were the gods themselves.

The kingdom of Osiris was called by the Egyptians the Fields of Aalu. Here the dead lived again a similar life to that which they had passed upon earth. It was a land of agriculture and of simple country pleasures. There the wheat grew to the height of five cubits, the ears being two cubits long, while the ears of barley were even larger. The South part contained the Lake of the *Kharu* fowl, in the North was the lake of the *Re* fowl. The whole territory was surrounded by an iron wall (chaps. cix and cxlix). The pictures represent a country intersected by canals which form islands. Here the deceased carries on his agricultural pursuits, he ploughs with a yoke of oxen, he drives the oxen over the ploughed field to tread in the seed, and he reaps the corn, which is as tall as himself. In another part he is paddling in a canoe on one of the canals, probably for pleasure as he carries his provisions with him (Papyrus of Nebseni). This existence, though ideal in some ways, was not altogether attractive to the ease-loving Egyptian. The hard manual work, to which the educated classes were unaccustomed, was distasteful, and yet the Fields of Peace, of which the Fields of Aalu were a part, were places of happiness and enjoyment. It was to remedy this one defect, that the models of servants were placed in the graves. Originally these were servants of all kinds, but they became stereotyped in the Middle Kingdom, after which time only the farm labourers, carrying hoe, pick, and basket, are found. These are known as *ushabti* figures. The inscription on them is an address from the deceased, in which he adjures them to take upon themselves the tasks which Osiris, ruler of the land to which he was going, might command him to perform.

I cannot refrain from quoting Plutarch on Osiris as god of the dead. "As to that circumstance of their mythology, which the priests of the present age seem to have in so much abhorrence, and of which they never speak but with the utmost caution and reserve, *that Osiris rules over the Dead, and is in reality none other than the Hades or Pluto of the Greeks*—'tis the not rightly apprehending in what manner this is true, which has given occasion to all the disturbance which has been raised upon this point ; filling the minds of the vulgar with doubts and suspicions, unable as they are to conceive, how the most pure and truly holy Osiris should have his dwelling under the earth, amongst the bodies of those who appear to be dead. And, indeed, this God is removed as far as possible from the earth, being not susceptible of the least stain or pollution whatever, and pure from all communication with such Beings as are liable to corruption and death. As therefore the souls of men are not able to participate of the divine nature, whilst they are thus encompassed about with bodies and passions, any farther than by those obscure glimmerings, which they may be able to attain unto, as it were in a confused dream, through means of philosophy—so when they are freed from these impediments, and remove into those purer and unseen regions, which are neither discernible by our present senses nor liable to accidents of any kind, 'tis then that this God becomes their leader and their king ; upon him they wholly depend, still beholding without satiety, and still ardently longing after that beauty, which 'tis not possible for man to express or think." (*Squire's translation.*)

34. *Osiris in the Sed-festival.* It has been observed by Herr Möller (*A.Z.* 1901, p. 71) that Osiris plays a large part in the ceremonies of the Sed-festival, and it is remarkable that the King himself represents the god. Of the kings thus depicted we have fourteen, though it is uncertain whether the sculptures of Sety I as Osiris are intended to represent the Sed-festival.

1. Narmer .	.	. Prehistoric	El-Kab .	Hierakonpolis, Pl. xxvi.
2. Zer .	.	. Ist Dyn.	Abydos	Royal Tombs.
3. Den .	.	. Ist Dyn.	Abydos	Royal Tombs.
4. Ra-en-user	.	. Vth Dyn.	Abusir	A.Z. 1899, Taf. I.
5. Pepy-Mery-Ra .		VIth Dyn.	Hammamat	. L.D. II, 115a.
6. Usertsen III (not contemporary).				
		XIIth Dyn.	Semneh .	. L.D. III, 48, 49, 51.
7. Amenhotep I		XVIIIth Dyn.	Karnak.	
8 Thothmes III .		,, ,,	Thebes. Semneh.	L.D. III, 36.
,, ,,		,, ,,	Abydos .	. Abydos II, Pl. xxxiii.
9. Amenhotep III		,, ,,	Thebes. Soleb	. L.D. III, 74.
10. Akhenaten	.	,, ,,	El Amarna	. L.D. III, 100.
11. Rameses I		. XIXth Dyn.	Qurna .	. L.D. III, 131.
12. Sety I.	.	,, ,,	Qurna .	. { Champollion II, 149. Rossellini III, 57. }
13. Rameses II	.	,, ,,	El Kab .	. L.D. III, 174.
,, ,,		,, ,,	Ehnasya.	
14. Osorkon II	.	. XXIInd Dyn.	Bubastis .	. Festival Hall of Osorkon II.

The latest representation, that of Osorkon, is the best preserved, and gives the ceremony in most detail. The King, robed as Osiris, and holding the crook and scourge, emblems of the god of the dead,

sometimes marches, sometimes is carried, in procession through the temple. He wears either the white crown or the red crown according to the part he has to play. During a portion of the ceremony he is accompanied by the queen and the princesses. The King however is the chief personage, and to him worship appears to be paid as to a god. Next in importance to him is the great figure of Upuaut of the South, which is carried by six priests immediately in front of the living representative of Osiris. The procession is headed by the *Mut neter en Siuti.* The Divine Mother of Him of Siut. " He of Siut " is a title of Upuaut as god of that city. Following the figure of Upuaut are two priests carrying small standards, one of Upuaut of the North, and one of the Joint of Meat which in Ptolemaic times is called Khonsu. This festival took place on the first day of Khoiak.

Of Rameses II, whose festivals exceeded in number those of any other king, I know only two representations. He is enthroned in a shrine and wears the white crown ; his son Kha-em-nast, who stands before him, "satisfies the heart of the Lord of the Two Lands at the Sed-festival." The date of this at El Kab is the forty-first year of the king's reign. Another instance of the Osiride king enthroned is found at Ehnasya.

Sety I is shown as an Osiride figure in a tomb at Thebes, but it is not certain that he is celebrating the Sed-festival, as he wears the Atef crown and not one of the crowns of Egypt. There is also a representation of him as Osiris in a shrine, with Ptah and Sekhet on one side, Amen-Ra and Mut on the other ; but again there is nothing to show that it is the Sed-festival.

Rameses I appears in the double shrine which forms the hieroglyph for the Sed-festival. The shrine is surmounted by the crouching hawk, and the king wears the white crown.

Akhenaten's Sed-festival is figured in the style peculiar to that king. He wears the red crown, and is borne on a litter by priests, while the sun's disk stretches down innumerable hands to bless him as he passes on his way. Here again there is a date : the 12th year, the second month of Pert (Mechir), the eighth day

Amenhotep III has left two records of his Sed-festival, one at Thebes and one at Soleb. At Thebes he is enthroned in the two shrines, and wears in one case the white crown, in the other the red crown. Before him is the emblem of the *Ka*, a staff with

In a little building within the enclosure of Karnak (PRISSE, *Monuments*, pls. xxxi-xxxiii, and DE ROUGÉ, *Mélanges d'Arch.* I, pp. 14-16) there are some sculptures of Tirhakah which give scenes from his Sed-festival. As it is a late example, variations are introduced; but still many of the characteristics remain. The standards of Upuaut and Thoth are carried by emblematic figures, but a new standard is introduced on which is the head of Hathor surmounted by the feather of Maat. She is called *nebt Sed*, " The lady of the Sed [festival]." A new feature in the ceremony is the raising of four gods on the *thes*-sign by a priest and the " divine wife of the god "; and in the procession of the arks of the gods, a woman, probably the queen, is a conspicuous figure. Another scene shows the king and queen performing a ceremony in the presence of Osiris, here represented as a sarcophagus out of which grows a tree. The king is throwing rings to the four points of the compass, and behind him are the three semi-circular objects which appear behind the dancing figures in the representations of Narmer and Den. The queen is of equal importance with the king in this ceremony, she shoots arrows to the four quarters of the compass. In this instance, the royal lady, who plays so large a part in the Sed-festival, is either the mother or the wife of the king, and not the daughter as in earlier times.

In the Ashmolean Museum there is an unpublished slab of Ptolemy I, who is represented with the insignia of Osiris and the sacred standards of the festival, the Ibis, the Hawk, the Joint of Meat, and the Jackal. It was found at Koptos (PETRIE, *Koptos*, p. 19.)

two human arms, surmounted by a hawk, which presents the notched palm-branch, emblem of millions of years, to the deified king. Over the arms of the *Ka* hangs the sign of Life attached to the signs of the Sed-festival. At Soleb he is seen standing, wearing the red crown, and accompanied by Queen Thyi and the *Seten Mesu*, Royal Children, i.e. the princesses. The standards carried in procession are five in number, that of Upuaut being foremost. He is also represented enthroned and wearing the red crown. The date of the festival appears to be in the month Khoiak.

Thothmes III recorded his Sed-festival at two places, Semneh and Abydos, or possibly they are the records of two separate festivals. At Abydos very little remains, only the figure of the enthroned king with his name, and in front of him the hide on a pole; some other fragments show that a priest in a panther-skin stood before him (PETRIE, *Abydos* ii, pl. xxxiii). At Semneh he is enthroned in a shrine, and wears the white crown, and before him are standards, the foremost one being that of " Upuaut, Leader of the South and the Two Lands," a title of Upuaut of the South. This is the only standard named. Behind the shrine the Osirified Thothmes appears again, standing and wearing the red crown ; and in another place he is again sitting, wearing the red crown and attended by the Anmutef priest.

The Sed-festival of Amenhotep I. is sculptured on a slab found at Karnak by M. Legrain. The king is enthroned, wearing the dress, and bearing the emblems, of Osiris.

At Semneh we have the Sed-festival of Usertsen III celebrated by Thothmes III, with, apparently, the same ritual as that of a living king. Usertsen is enthroned in a shrine which is carried in a boat. He wears the white crown, and before him are the standards of Upuaut, Neith, the Joint of Meat, and the Ibis, carried by emblems of Life and Strength. The standard of Neith is actually foremost, but it appears to take that place to fill the gap below the standard of Upuaut, which projects very far forward.

Pepy I has left many records of his Sed-festivals, but as far as I know there is only one representation, which is cut on the rocks at Hammamat. He is figured in the double shrine, on one side wearing the white crown, on the other side with the red crown. Below is an inscription, " The first time of the Sed-festival." Another graffito tells us that the

festival took place in his 18th year, on the 27th day of the 3rd month of Shemu (Epiphi).

Of Ra-en-user's Sed-festival only fragments of the sculpture remain. The king wears the white crown, but of the standards carried before him all are destroyed, except one, the Joint of Meat. In another fragment are the *Seten Mesut*, Royal Daughters, carried in litters which resemble sedan-chairs.

King Den's Sed-festival is recorded on a small ebony tablet found at Abydos. He is enthroned in a shrine, and wears the double crown. The dancing figure in front I take to be another scene in the same ceremony ; as in the case of Thothmes III, where the king, vested as Osiris, stands immediately behind the figure of himself enthroned.

King Zer appears twice enthroned, once with the white crown, once with the red crown. In each case the standard of Upuaut precedes him.

The earliest representation of this festival, where the king appears as Osiris, is on the great mace-head of Narmer. The king is enthroned in a shrine raised on a flight of nine steps, and wears the red crown. The scene before him is divided into three registers ; in the first are the four sacred standards, that of Upuaut being foremost ; in the second and principal register are three dancers, and a litter like a sedan-chair, containing a figure closely wrapped up, which we know from the sculptures of Ra-en-user to be the *Seten Mest*, Royal Daughter. Below there are cattle and numerals. In these scenes we get the earliest representation of this ceremony, and we can see that the principal points are preserved down to the last occasion of which we have any record, viz. Osorkon II, a period extending over four thousand years. The points are three in number :—

1. The king in the robe, and with the emblems, of Osiris, evidently representing the god.

2. The importance of the sacred standards, and the prominent position of the standard of Upuaut.

3. The presence of the Royal Daughters as an integral part of the ceremony.

As to the second point, some explanation may be found when we turn to the name of the festival, of which there has as yet been no satisfactory derivation. On the Palermo Stone there is a record, in the eleventh year of an unnamed king (called König V by Dr. Schäfer), of the birth of the god Sed, the name being determined by the figure which, in later times, is called Upuaut, a jackal on a

F

pedestal, and in front of him the ostrich feather, emblem of space and lightness, on which, according to Professor Sethe, the king ascended into heaven at his death. In the tomb of Kaa (MAR. *Mast.* D. 19), and also in another tomb found at Sakkara by Mariette, hitherto unpublished, the deceased is said to have been " the divine servant of the god Sed," with the same determinative as on the Palermo Stone. If the Sed-festival were in honour of the jackal-god Sed, it would be natural that the figure of the jackal should take a prominent place in the ceremonies. It is remarkable that in the later sculptures of this scene, the jackal standard is often carried by an emblematic figure, an *ankh* or an *uas-sceptre* with arms.

Herr Möller has published some curious scenes from a coffin found at Deir el Bahri (*A.Z.* 1901, p. 71), in which the Sed-festival is depicted, but without any royal name. The Royal Daughters and the standards of Upuaut are represented as in the cases already cited; Upuaut is called Lord of Siut and Leader of the South, and the ostrich feather in front of the stand has been metamorphosed into a lotus. The closely wrapped figures in litters have the names Amset, Hapi, and Duamutef, there is nothing but their likeness to similar figures at Abusir and on the mace-head of Narmer, to show that they are intended for the princesses; further on, however, there are other figures in the same attitude and attire, though not in litters, who are labelled *Seten Mesut.* The scene of driving four calves is not known elsewhere in the Sed-festival, though it is not uncommon in other representations of the worship of the gods.

35. *The Da-seten-hetep formula.*—There is one curious point to be noticed in the very common funerary formula Da-seten-hetep; we find that in the Old Kingdom Osiris is seldom mentioned. I give a table made up from Lepsius' *Denkmäler*, Mariette's *Mastabas*, Davis' *Mastaba of Akhethetep*, and *Rock Tombs of Sheikh Said.*

	IVth.	Vth.	VIth.	Total.
Anubis alone . .	15	23	23	61
Anubis and Osiris .	1	8	13	22
Osiris alone . .	1	2	1	4
Anubis with other gods	1	1	1	3
Formula without a god	1	3	1	5
Total . .	19	37	39	95

By Anubis I mean the couchant jackal-god, who appears without name, and with the title Khenti-Neter-seh.

It is evident from this table that it is not to Osiris that the prayer is addressed, and I think that the reason is as follows:

I have shown that the king, when living, is identified with Osiris in the Sed-festival, that he was identified after death with the same god is proved by the coffin of Men-kau-Ra, where the dead king is called "the Osiris Men-kau-Ra;" and also by the pyramid texts. There is a litany in the Pyramid of Unas (l. 209, *et seq.*), which apostrophizes Osiris by various epithets, and continues, "If he lives, Unas lives; if he does not die, neither does Unas die; if he is not destroyed, Unas is not destroyed; if he begets not, Unas begets not; if he begets, then Unas begets." And it closes with the words, "Thy body is the body of Unas; thy flesh is the flesh of Unas; thy bones the bones of Unas; as thou art, so is Unas; as is Unas, so art thou." In the Pyramid of Teta (l. 256) there is the very definite statement that "this Teta is Osiris."

Here, then, we see that, alive or dead, the King is Osiris and Osiris is the King. He is the incarnate god upon earth to whom all prayers are addressed, and who, in connection with Anubis and other gods of the dead, looks after the welfare of those who have passed out of life. Therefore it would be mere vain repetition and tautology to introduce the name of Osiris in the funerary prayers when he has already been addressed under the title of *Seten* (king). As time advanced this appears to be forgotten, and gradually the name of Osiris is inserted, and that of Anubis ousted, till finally the King and Osiris, one and the same person, are mentioned together, often to the exclusion of any other god, in the prayers for the dead.

There is one example which goes to prove my argument, and which shows that even as late as the XVIIIth Dynasty the origin of the formula was not completely forgotten. The inscription is on a wooden statue (CHAMP. Not. ii, pp. 719, 720), and runs thus: "May the king grant an offering," then come the titles and name of Queen Aahmes-Nefertari, "may she give life, strength, and health, for the *ka* of," and then follow the titles and name of the deceased. Here, then, are the incarnate god and the deified queen named together as the givers of what is necessary in the next world.

36. *Ceremonies in honour of Osiris.*—There are

several other ceremonies in honour of Osiris, which cannot be classified under any of the foregoing heads.

Plutarch mentions two which are very similar and may possibly be the same ceremony as practised in different parts of the country. At the one which takes place at the winter solstice, " they lead the sacred cow in procession seven times round her temple, which procession they call in express terms " The Searching after Osiris." The other " doleful rite " was to expose to public view "a gilded Ox covered with a pall of the finest black linen (for this animal is regarded as the living image of Osiris), and this ceremony they perform four days successively, beginning on the seventeenth of the abovementioned month (Athyr)."

The festival of lights is mentioned in the Ritual of Dendereh, and is described by Herodotus. " There shall be celebrated a voyage on the 22nd of Khoiak in the 8th hour of the day, when many lamps shall be lighted near them (the relics) and the gods belonging to them, the list of whose names runs thus, Horus, Thoth, Anubis, Isis, Nephthys, and the nineteen Children of Horus. These shall be put into 34 boats. Furthermore these gods shall be bandaged with the four webs from the South Town and the North Town (Sais)" (BRUGSCH). Herodotus describes the festival as he saw it at Sais. " When they meet to sacrifice in the city of Sais, they hang up by night a great number of lamps, filled with oil and a mixture of salt, round every house, the tow swimming on the surface. These burn the whole night, and the Festival is thence named *The Lighting of Lamps.* The Egyptians, who are not present at this solemnity observe the same ceremonies wherever they be, and lamps are lighted that night, not only in Sais, but throughout all Egypt. Nevertheless, the reasons for using these illuminations and paying so great respect to this night are kept secret." There are many allusions to this custom scattered through the religious texts, and all show that it was a ceremony in honour of Osiris. " O, Osiris, I kindle the flame for thee on the day of the shrouding of thy mummified body." (*Stela of Rameses IV*, PIEHL, *A.Z.*, 1885, 16). " The flame for thy *ka*, O Osiris Khenti-Amentiu, the flame for thy *ka*, O chief *Kheri-heb* Petamenap . . It protects thee and shines about thy head . . . . . it makes all thine enemies to fall down before thee, thine enemies are overthrown " (DÜMICHEN, *A.Z.*, 1883, 14-15). At Soleb

during the Sed-festival of Amenhotep III, the lighting of a lamp forms part of the function (L. *D.* iii, 84) ; and at an earlier period still, in the XIIth Dynasty, the kindling of a spark or lamp was evidently one of the chief rites at the commemorative ceremonies for the dead (GRIFFITH, *Siut*, pl. viii).

Herodotus mentions a ceremony which he describes partly from observation and partly from hearsay, but which seems to be a confused account of some Osirian rite. " The Egyptians celebrate a certain festival from the day of Rampsinitus' descent (into Hades) to that of his re-ascension . . . . . . The priests every year at that time, clothing one of their order in a cloak woven the same day, and covering his eyes with a mitre, guide him into the way that leads towards the Temple of Ceres [Isis], and then return, upon which, they say, two wolves come and conduct him to the Temple, twenty stades distant from the city, and afterwards accompany him back to the place from whence he came." The garment woven in one day is probably the same that is ordered in the Ritual of Dendereh, " the 19th of Khoiak, on which day shall be made the linen for wrapping the body." The two wolves stand for Upuaut of the South and Upuaut of the North coming from the temple of Isis to meet the incarnate Osiris. They conduct him as the " openers of roads."

Firmicus Maternus gives a description of a ceremony which apparently represents the burial rites of Osiris. A pine tree was cut down, and the heart of the tree removed. From this was made an image of Osiris, which was replaced in the hollow tree as in a tomb, where it remained till the following year, when it was burned.

CHAPTER VI.

THE GRAFFITI.

37. The walls of the Sety Temple have been used for many centuries to record the scribblings of visitors. The modern tourist, who scratches his name on the wall of an ancient building, rouses our ire and makes us indignant ; but when the graffito is over fifteen hundred years old it becomes hallowed by time, and we hasten to copy it. During the Greek and Roman periods, the Sety Temple was a place of pilgrimage, as the engraved footprints show.

There was an oracle of Bes in one of the side chambers, and those who consulted the oracle slept one night in the temple, and the dreams that they dreamt on that night were supposed to be the answer of the God. The names of these anxious inquirers are scratched thickly on the walls of the staircase and corridor of the Bull, and the small chamber of Osiris, but more sparsely elsewhere.

In Coptic times the temple was used as a nunnery, and the walls are covered, in many places, with inscriptions in the characteristic red paint of the Copts. The greater number are in the pillared chamber (called *Z* in the plan in Caulfeild's *Temple of the Kings*), but, like the Greek graffiti, they are to be found in other parts of the building. Some had faded almost away during the time that the temple was used as a Christian Church, and fresh inscriptions had been painted over them. No. 16 was a palimpsest of this kind, one inscription being in black, the other in red. The black was not so permanent as the red, and had vanished almost entirely. It could only be seen when the wall itself was in shade and the sun shining fully on the wall at right angles to it. Then by sitting as close as possible to the wall and looking along it, the letters were seen like shadows by the reflected light. I have copied about half the Coptic inscriptions in the temple and not a third of the others. Professor Sayce copied all the Greek, Karian, and Phoenician graffiti and published some, though not in facsimile. Mr. Garstang (*El Arabah*) published in facsimile some of the graffiti in the small chambers of Osiris, Isis, and Horus. This is all that has been done for the Greek graffiti. Of the Coptic inscriptions, M. Bouriant is, I think, the only person who has published any, and those were hand copies, not facsimiles.

38. Hieratic graffiti. Graffiti in hieratic are rare in the Temple of Sety. They are inscribed in red on blank spaces on the walls. The first is in the chapel of Ptah, the second in the corridor of the Bull.

Mr. Griffith's translation and notes are as follows:
1. "King of Upper and Lower Egypt .
chief prophet of Amonrasonther, son of the Sun, Lord of Crowns, the leader Psebkhane (Psusennes) beloved of Amonrasonther (?). The chief prophet of Amonrasonther . . . Pasebkhane, beloved of Amon."

There is no proper end to the cartouche, and it is rather extraordinary in itself. Perhaps one might cut it down to ⬡, considering the other signs as superfluous.

2. "The king of Upper and Lower Egypt who hath made a monument in the house of his maker; he hath builded . . . . for his father Osiris. The scribe Pshasu, who came with the scribe ”

39. PL. XXII. The Phoenician graffiti are roughly scratched on the walls, even more roughly than the Greek. Professor Müller of Vienna has very kindly looked at them and has given a tentative translation of No. 1. "Ich[bin] Ebdosiris . . . . der Mächtige aus (?) Hazta (?)."

The figures given on this plate are scratched on the blank walls of the passage which contains the Tablet of Abydos. These unfinished walls offer a good field for graffiti of all kinds, and visitors to the temple appear to have availed themselves of the space afforded. I have given only a few specimens. Abraxas, the Gnostic deity, appears as a Roman soldier with a staff in his hand. The mounted soldier is remarkable for the ingenious manner in which the artist has made the bridle form part of the horse's head.

40. Greek graffiti. The Greek graffiti are described by Mr. Grafton Milne as follows:

The copies made last winter by Miss Eckenstein are reproduced in facsimile on PLS. XXI, XXIII, and XXIV. They form a supplement to those copied by Mr. Garstang in 1900, which I edited in chap. vi of his volume on El-Arabah (Quaritch, 1901): and the remarks there given in preface may be applied here. It may be added that only one of the present instalment is included among those published by Professor Sayce, but many appear in the plates of the Corpus Inscriptionum Semiticarum prepared from Théodule Deveria's note-books. A comparison of the latter plates with the recent copies suggests that the surface of the stones in the great staircase has suffered an appreciable amount of damage in the last forty years.

1. I am unable to obtain any connected sense out of these letters. In the second line Σικ[υ]ώνιος, in a hand of the 3rd cent. B.C., may be read.

Chapel of Amen: South wall.

2. Ἀρίστις | ἀφίκετο· | Τίμαρ|χος· | Νότιος· | Δρόμων. 2nd cent. B.C.

Chamber Z : South wall.

3. Ἰ<σ>σωρίων Πλουτογένευ[ς]. 2nd cent. B.C.

Corridor of Kings : East wall.

4(a). Ἀπολλώνιος Πτολεμαίου. 2nd cent. B.C.

4(b). Τὸ προσκύνη(μα) Ἀπολλωνίας. 2nd cent. B.C.

Chapel of Amen : North wall.

5. Ἐπικράτης | Νικολάου. 3rd cent. B.C.

Chapel of Amen.

6. L λή Μεχ(ε)ι[ρ] (or Μεχ(εὶρ) ί) | Ἡράκλειτος
Πυλεμάρχ[ου] | Ἀχαῖος ἀφίκετο. 2nd cent. B.C.
The date is probably to be referred to the
38th year of Ptolemy Euergetes II.

Chapel of Amen : West wall.

7. Ἀριστοκλῆς. 2nd cent. B.C.

Cella of Osiris : on throne, to left.

8(a). Το προσκύνημα Σαβέινου Μυρίνου (?). 2nd
cent. A.D.

8(b). Τμεησολλ (?) | Ζαζέλμις ἔκει. 2nd cent. B.C.
For the name Ζαζέλμις—a Thracian form
—cf. Ἀθλουζέλμις Κότυος, El Arabah, c. vi.
No. 30.

8(c). Ἀρτεμίδωρος ἥκω ἐπὶ σω[τη]ρίᾳ. 1st cent B.C.
The formula ἐπὶ σωτηρίᾳ recurs in No. 19,
and in Sayce's article, p. 381, note, and p. 382.

8(d). Ἀθηναγόρας Ζωμοψηχ . ος ἥκω ἔτους κ κ γ.

8(e). Δαμήτριος (?) Ἀλεξανδρεὺς ἥκω. 1st cent. B.C.

8(f). Ἀ]φθόνητος Ἀττίνου Θεσσαλος ἥκω. 2nd cent.
B.C.
(I have disregarded the casual letters between 8(e) and 8(f), and on the left-hand
above).

9. Τὸ πριοκύνημα (l. προσκύνημα) Δημητρίου. 2nd
cent. B.C.

10. The four letters left do not give any clue to the
sense.

Cella of Osiris : on throne, to right.

11. Φιλοκράτης | .κιθ[. . .] . . 1st cent. A.D.

12. [Φιλ]οκλῆς Σεουετρι προσκυνῶν χαίρειν λέγω.
Φιλοκλῆς Ἱεροκλέους Τροιζήνιος παρεγενήθην προσ-
κυνῶν τὸν Σάρα[π]ιν τ ι ν | ἐπὶ πης (l. τῆς)
Ἀβύδου πολιορκίας. L 5′ Παηνι (l. Παυνὶ) κη′.
1st cent. B.C.
The latter part of the graffito is given by
Sayce, p. 381, who reads παρεγενέθην—ἐπὶ τῆς
—L κ′Παυνὶ κη′. He considers the siege
mentioned in the inscription to have been in

the rising suppressed by Ptolemy Epiphanes :
but I should date the writing to the latter
part of the 1st cent. B.C., possibly the reign of
Augustus ; and the siege may be connected
with the Ethiopian invasion of the Thebaid
in 24 B.C. The conclusion drawn from this
graffito by P. Meyer (das Heerwesen der
Ptolemäer u. Römer in Aegypten, p. 59, note
201), that the siege marked the downfall of
the worship of Sarapis at Abydos, is certainly
unfounded.

The stray letters at the top of the graffito
seem to be mere scribblings : as possibly are
also the five letters under the second line.

13. Τὸ προσκύνημα Ἡρακλοῦ[ς] Ἡρῶνος μητρὸς
Σεραπύγχιος ἀπὸ Ἀντινουπολέως.
Τὸ προσκύνημα Δημητρίου ευλατοχου(?) καὶ
Ποτάμωνος πατρὸς καὶ Δημητρίου ἀδελφῶν.
2nd cent. A.D.

Corridor of the bull : North wall.

14. Καπῶνος καὶ Δημᾶτος | τὸ προσκύνημα ὧδε. 2nd
cent. B.C.
C.I.Sem. vol. i. pl. xvi. No. 53 ; on this
plate is shown to the right a further graffito
ΠΡΩΤΑΡΧΟΥΤΟΠΡ.

15. Θεόφιλος [ι]ατρός.
C.I.Sem. vol. i. pl. xvi. 55. The copy
given on this plate shows the ι of ιατρός as
legible.

16. Ἱμουπβύκης.
C.I.Sem. vol. i. pl. xvi. 54.

Staircase : beneath king's collar, on body.

17(a). Νι[κις Κυρηναῖος].
Ἀλ[καῖος]
ακ (retrograde)
Ἀρμ[όδιος Ὀδησιτής]
Μενεκράτει υτυκειν (l. εὐτυχεῖν). 3rd cent. B.C.
C.I.Sem. vol. i. pl. xvi. 27. The read-
ings given there are much fuller. (1)
ΝΙΚΙΣΚΥ (2) ΛΛΚΑΙΟΣ (3) ΚΥ (pre-
sumably the letters copied as ΑΑ here) (4)
ΑΘΑΝΙΠΠΟΣΑΡΓΕΙΟΣ (a line which
seems to have entirely disappeared) (5)
ΑΡΜΟΔΙΟΣΟΔΗΣΙΤΗΣ (6) ΜΕΝΕΚ-
ΡΑΤΕΙΕΥΤΥΧΕΙΝ

Staircase : right hand, on curved second block.

17(b). Ἡρακλῆς. 2nd cent. B.C.

Staircase : next block.

18(a). Σουαβὼ|ις . | τα. 2nd cent. B.C.

    C.I.Sem. vol. i. pl. xvi. No. 4. The second line is not given in Deveria's copy. The third line is possibly an independent scribble.

18(b). Λητοδώριος | ὁ θεὸς | *Ώρις (? l. *Ώρος). 3rd cent. B.C.

    C.I.Sem. vol. i. pl. xvi. 4. The reading there given in the first line is ΛΗΤΟΔΩΡΟΣ. The graffito is somewhat mixed up on the left with No. 18(a).

18(c). Τωγὴς· | Παμρᾶς· | Νααραῦς· (ς) Πετ|[ωσῖρις]. 2nd cent. B.C.

    C.I.Sem. vol. i. pl. xvi. 4. The fourth line, omitted in the present copy, is. supplied by the previous one.

Staircase : right hand, on upper second block.

19. Παραγέγονεν Ἀγάθεινος ἐπὶ σωτη ρίᾳ · παρεγέ[νε]το δε καὶ Δημήτρ[ιος]| ᾦ παρωνύμιον Ἴλλαυς καὶ Ὀνυσία κ[αὶ] ἡ θυγάτηρ Χαρ[ι]σεστρῖτη σὺν Παρσπ[. . .]| τὸ (l. τῷ) π[α]ιδι κη (l. καὶ) Μύρζω καὶ υἱὸς Πέπτιξ. 2nd cent. B.C.

    C.I.Sem. vol. i. pl. xvi. 6. Deveria's copy, as there given, differs in several points from the present one. Above the beginning of the first line it shows ΛΔ : at the end of the first line it reads ΕΠΙCΩΤΗΡ : in the second, ΗΛΙ——ΔΗΜΗΤΡΙΟ : in the third, ΚΑΛΛΑΥС for ΙΛΛΑΥС : in the fourth,—ΧΑΡΙСΕСΤΡΑΤΗΩΙΠΠΑΡΗ : at the end of the fifth, ΥΙΟΙΤΕΤΤΙΞ. It is difficult to decide as to the respective merits of the readings in the later lines, which are mainly concerned with non-Hellenic names.

20(a). Ἀβλουθίης Χυσιτης. 2nd cent. B.C.

    C.I.Sem. vol. i. pl. xvi. 2. In this plate the name ΑΒΛΟΥΘΙΗС is shown repeated at the end of the second line.

Staircase : North side, in front of the king's staff.

21(b). τὸ προσκ(ύνημα)· ἥκω κατάγ(ων ?). 1st cent. B.C.

21(c). Διονύσιος | [Κ]αλλιχάρους. 3rd cent. B.C.

    C.I.Sem. vol. i. pl. xvii. 18. The initial Κ of the second line is there given.

21(e). Δ[.]ιας ἥκω | [εἰς Ἀβυ]δον μετὰ | [Ἀριστί]ππου. 2nd cent. B.C.

    C.I.Sem. vol. i. pl. xvii. 21. The graffito is there given in full as ΕΡΜΙΑСΗΚΩ | ΕΙСΑΒΥΔΟΝΜΕΤΑ | ΑΡΙСΤΙΠΠΟΥ.

This reading does not however account for the initial Δ shown in the present copy.

21(f). [Π]ατεαρβεσχῦ[ις] | Πατοῦτος καλῆς | κ[α]ὶ τυ[ὺς] ἀδελφο|ύς. 2nd cent. B.C.

    C.I.Sem. vol. i. pl. xvii. No. 17. Deveria's reading, as there given, is fuller in the first and third lines than the present one : his copy shows (1) ΠΕΤΕΗΡΒΕСΧΙΝΙС (3) ΚΑΙΤΟΥСΑΒΛΕΛΦΟ.

21(g). Ἐ[ρ]μῖνις· | Τυκοιόις. 1st cent B.C.

Staircase : right hand, first block.

22(b). Ἀβλουθίης. 2nd cent. B.C.

    C.I.Sem. vol. i. pl. xvi. 24. The name, which is Thracian, recurs in No. 20(a) : cf. Ἀβλουζέλμις Κότυος, *El Arabah*, c. vi. No. 30.

Staircase : South wall.

23(a). Νεοπτόλεμος Μ[. .]ρου κασεπ . . . . . 2nd cent. B.C.

23(b). Πυθόδωρος. 2nd cent. B.C.

                   J. GRAFTON MILNE.

§ 41.—COPTIC GRAFFITI &c.

(PLATES XXV—XXXVII.)

The numerous graffiti to be seen in the temple of Seti[1] show not only that the building was at some period frequented by Christians, but that one chamber at least (Z, in S. Wing) was employed by them for some special purpose ; for on its walls and pillars alone were collected more than half the total of our texts. Whether this chamber served as a chapel we cannot learn ; to-day no remains of Christian building are traceable in the temple precincts, to show whether a church or monastery ever occupied the spaces about the ancient walls and columns. Although it is evident that most of the texts were written by or for women—male names do not occur except in the lists of saints or clerical dignitaries—they give no clear indication as to where the writers dwelt. One (or more) monasteries are indeed mentioned or implied ; perhaps that " of *Tbouliané* " or Belyana in B. 11 ; while "the people of *Pertês*" (Bardis) occur in No. 26. The neigh-

---

[1] Many were copied by Bouriant (here B.) in 1884-85 and published in *Mission franç.* l. 382 ff. New copies of some of these are given by Miss Murray.

bouring monastery of Moses however, as the *Dair* to the West of the temple appears to be now named,[1] recalls the saint so prominently invoked in the graffiti (*v.* especially 19, 36, B. 11). This Moses is called by Makrizi[2] a native of Belyanâ. Presumably he is identical with the monastic hero who, with his brethren, wrecked the still surviving heathen temple at Abydos[3] (*Ebôt*) and whose career is made to fall somewhere between the death of Shenoute (451) and the accession of the patriarch Theodosius (536).[4] But whether this person is the same with the archimandrite—likewise subsequent to Shenoute[5]—who addressed epistles to a community of nuns[6] and composed a 'canon,'[7] has not been demonstrated. The fact that our graffiti name various female officials of a convent, points at any rate to a nun's community in the neighbourhood. But to what period the texts should be assigned it is not easy to determine. Moses indeed is often referred to as an already recognized saint. But only one text allows of precise determination : B. 11 records Gabriel as the archbishop, thus in all probability indicating the beginning of the 10th century. B. 13 perhaps mentions a visit of Pesynthius of Coptos, which would be in about the years 600—620 ; this, however, is quite uncertain. Arguments drawn from the palæographical features of such rough inscriptions can not at present have much value.

The sequence of the graffiti in the plates is due to considerations of size and space. According to contents they can be grouped and are here described as follows[8] : Scriptural quotations (protective charms), invocations &c., proper names with accompanying prayers, names only, texts referring to the rise of the river.[9] The last of these groups is especially interesting but not wholly intelligible.
[1, 2, 23, 26, 3, 14, 27, 10, 31, 24, 12, 11, 32, 25, 7,

8, 9, 20, 30, 16, 18, 4, 5, 29, 39, 28, 36, 48, 33, 37, B. 12, 19, 43, 41, 49, 35, 40, 21, 34, B. 3, B. 4, B. 11, 42, 13, 6, 44, 38, 47, B. 13, B. 15, B. 17, B. 16, 22, 17, 15, 45, 46.]

1.—*Z*, E. Wall (= B. 2, 8, 9, 10). The 2 ll. in small characters above are the first and last verses of St. Matthew (i. 1, xxviii. 20) and St. Luke (i. 1, xxiv. 50, 51). The next 2 ll., continued in the broken text on right, show St. Mark i. 1 and xiv. 18*b*, 19, 20. The short ll., following the cross (*anok eis*), are the beginning of Christ's letter to Abgar. These texts were all familiar in Christian Egypt as protective charms and are often found written upon the walls of dwellings.[10]

2.—*Z*, W. Wall. (= B. 7). The names (*naine nran*) of the Apostles and the beginnings and ends of the Gospels of Matthew and Luke, as in No. 1. The rough 'orans' above the text bears the name '*Martha* the little'; in the blank below the text are *Tsabina*, *Tamanne* and other, illegible names.

23.—*Z*, E. Wall. (= B. 6). Invokes God the Father, the 'seven holy angels' (five archangels are named) and enumerates the twelve Apostles (= Mt. x. 2, omitting Thomas). Ll. 16 ff. perhaps a prayer that 'the people of our . . .' (*nrôme mpe*[*nnet*[11]]) may be preserved 'from all ill' (*eppethoou nim*).

26.—*Z*, N. Wall. (= B. 5). List of women's names (ll. 1—9) followed by a prayer. '*Mekalou*[12] the little of *Pertês*,[13] *Tsenthôtrake*[14] of *Pertês*, *Patrekou*[15] the little, her sister, *Geôrgia* her mother, *Anastou*[16] the little, her sister, *Metretôre*[17] the little, their sister, *Marou*[18] their mother, [the la]dy (? *κυρά*) *Loule*[19] the little, . . . *nia*, her mother. Lord God Almighty (*παντοκ.*), watch (= *roeis*) thou over all the people of *Pertês*, small and great, within and without. Jesus have mercy on them all. *Mekalou.*'

3.—*Z*, broken pillar. (= B. 1 *cf.* B. 17). A Prayer. 'I . . . thee, . . . , I bless thee, Father, I bless thee, Son, I bl[ess] thee, Holy Ghost. I glorify thee and [I] give thee thanks (*εὐχαριστεῖν*). Iea, Iea, Iô, Adôn[ai], Ab[ras]a[x], Elôei, Sabaôth,

---

[1] Murray, *Handbook*[9], 747. The *Synaxarium*, 7th Bermudah, speaks of the mon. of Belyana as that of Moses.
[2] No. 59 in list of monasteries. Abû Ṣâliḥ f. 81*a* places it to the W. of Belyana, which would suit the present monastery.
[3] *Mission franç.* iv. 686. *Cf.* ? 'Moses and his brethren,' invoked on some stelae (*Rev. ég.* iv. 7, *Rec.* v. 63).
[4] The former, dying, foretells M.'s fame (*Miss.* iv. 682), while M. in turn prophecies of Theodosius, Severus and Anthimus (*l.c.* 688).
[5] M. quotes him (*l.c.* 695 &c.).
[6] *L.c.* 693 ff.
[7] Paris MS. copte 129[15], 14 (title only, so perhaps = the epistles, as sometimes with Shenoute).
[8] B. = texts published by Bouriant, *l.c.* and not copied by Miss Murray. The stelae, wine-jar and ostracon published here likewise come from Abydos.
[9] Other documents recording the river's rise : Krall, *Rechtsurk.* No. I. 25, Rainer *Führer* 1894, No. 618.

[10] *Cf.* Expl. Fund, *Arch. Report*, 1897-98, pp. 63, 67.
[11] *V.* No. 25.
[12] = Μεγαλοῦς or Μεγαλῶ.
[13] = Today *Bardis*, about 8 mi. N. of Abydos.
[14] *Lit.* 'The daughter of Theodorakios.'
[15] ? Fem. of Patricius.
[16] ? Fem. of Anastasius.
[17] = Μητροδώρα.
[18] *Cf.* Μαρούς, BGU. 232.
[19] Loula, Loulou, Λουλοῦς is generally masculine.

Almighty (παντοκράτωρ), ...; [who] fillest the heaven [and] the earth ; whom no place may contain ; who [sittest] upon [the] chariot (ἅρμα) of the Cherubim ; for the honour of whose glory the Seraphim do . . . their wings; whose might (κράτος) thousands of [thousands and ten thou]sands of ten thousands of angels (ἄγγελος) and archangels (ἀρχαγγ.) and authorities (ἐξουσία) and powers (ἤομι) and thrones (θρόνος) and dominions do obey (ὑποτάσσειν), worshipping (προσκυνεῖν) his holy glory, blessing him and his beloved son, Jesus Christ our Lord, and his Holy Spirit, crying out without pause, saying : Holy (ἅγιος), holy, holy, Lord (ͼͼ = κε), Sabaoth. Heaven and earth are full of thy holy glory.' I call on thee, Lord, God, Alm[ighty] (παντοκ.), the Fa[ther of] our Lord Jesus Christ ; Jesus the . . . . the Onlybegotten (μονογενής), Jesus the . . . . Father . . . . .
    Probably continued by No. 14.
    14.—Z, pillar. Probably continues No. 3. ' . . help (? r-βοηθός) . . .,' ' . . . my wretched soul and have mercy on me in the hour of need (ἀνάγκη), when I come forth from . . ., and give me means to (ti-thé nai) meet (? ἀπ[αντᾶν]) . . . without fear (hate). For every spirit (πνα nim[1]) . . . Forgiveness (pkô ebol) is . . .' Thellou is probably the writer's (fem.) name.[2]
    27.—Z, fallen pillar. A Prayer to Christ, similar to (perhaps connected with) Nos. 3, 14. ' Jesus, my . . .' is several times repeated and the words 'guide [me'] (r-hême), 'watch over me' (roeis ͼ[r]ͼôi), '[the ad]versary' (ἀντικείμενος, 'my end' (tahaê), 'thy kingdom' (tekmenterô) are legible.
    10.—Chamber below Corr. of Kings, little Wall. Ll. 1—8 (?) a prayer or invocation (cf. B. 17, beginning), naming the Virgin (παρθένος) and the archangel Ap[a Micha]el. ' . . . stretching forth (? sobtn) of thy hand. The others . . . . ., men and the cattle live and . . . . . thereon. Who sitteth upon (hmoo[s ah]rai) . . . . . the] Seraphim spread [3] [their wings . . .' L. 12 seems commemorative (anok . . τολαίπωρος). L. 16, perhaps a fresh text, records an event ' in this month Thoot.'
    31.—Z, E. Wall. ' The prayer [? of . . .' It addresses the Lord God Almighty. Legible are · ' . . . the heaven, who goeth in . . .' (? petbék ahoun), 'holy souls ', 'thy (? pek-) servant,' ' keep

the . . .' (harch ap-), 'without offence' (ejn σκανδαλον). Below, in smaller script, traces of various names, including Apa Moses.
    24.—Outer Court, pillar D. Names: Victor ' their brother,' Tsophia, Tsalamanna [4] and . . ., with prayer for their safety ([ek]ahareh eron apethoou nim). The nêt (v. No. 12) is named in l. 1. Letters of an older inscription also visible.
    12.—Z, N. Wall. Prayer (?) to the Almighty (? παντοκ.) on behalf of . . . . . 'and all their household ' (neurôme têrou), among them Tômanna (or Tamanna [5]) ' the head (tape) of the nût,'[6] Metredôra, Staurou. L. 9 ? pestauros etouaab. End ? rek nteumaaje.
    11.—Z, E. Wall. Prayer on behalf of the same persons (including tape nnêt) as in No. 12.
    32.—Z, N. Wall. Monogram at end probably Biktôr (Victor). Smaller, earlier text : ' Touêrt (?) the little.'
    25.—Z, S. Wall. Ll. 1—3, women's names, ? ['those of] our nêt,' Stephanou &c.; 4 ff., prayer to God Almighty to ' preserve them from all ill.' L. 10 ? 'Apa Moses,' followed by more names. Some here and in several other graffiti add the humble êôm ' little.'
    7.—Z, S. Wall. ' Theoucharis the little.'
    8.—Z, S. Wall. Prayer to 'the Lord God, the good Saviour,' for protection against all evil.
    9.—Chapel of Amon, N. Wall. Beginning of a prayer and of a name, κυρά . . .
    20.—Z, N. Wall. Name : ' Patrekoui (cf. No. 26) the little,' and prayer to God.
    30.—Z, E. Wall. Prayer by (?) [Metr]edôra the little (sêm) on behalf of ' Kollouthos, her dear little brother.'
    16.—Z, N. Wall. Middle group : ' Apa Sabinos the archimandrite. Lord God Almighty, watch over these (lit. the men) ' of our nêt.'[7] To left : in the names Tanin, Eulepou (? Eulogiou), Metretore (Mêtrodôra), figures of ' orantes ' and of two birds beside a plant (a frequent motive in Byzantine art, e.g. Cairo Catal. gén., Copt. Mons., pll. xlvii, xlviii). To right : in earlier text, name Tealia (?) ; in later, Tetras (or Antetras), Hrômanne.
    18.—Outer Court, pillar D. ' The holy Apa Sabinos.' Cf. No. 16.

----
[4] V. Crum, Copt. Ostr. 450.
[5] V. Cairo 8698.
[6] An unknown word, unless the same as that designating a building to be sold, in the deed Br. Mus., Or. 4883. Here it may be the convent or congregation. Cf. Nos. 11, 16, 24, 25.
[7] V. No. 12.

----
[1] Or ' For mercy . . .'
[2] Cf. Crum, Copt. Ostr., Ad. 38.
[3] Hrp; cf. hr*prep. But I can not read what follows.

4.—Outer Court, pillar D. Names: *Shenoute* the little, the lady (κυρά) *Ma[r]ou* the little . . . . .

5.—Outer Court, pillar C. Names: *Tsone* (= *Tsóne*), *Elisabêt*.

29.—*Z*, N. Wall. Name: *Kasta*.

39.—*Z*, W. Wall. Names: '*Joanna* the daughter of .

28.—*Z*, pillar. Beginning of a prayer: 'Lord God Almighty . . .' L. 5, 'bless us '

36.—*Z*, E. Wall. An Invocation of various saints. ' Holy (? ἅγια) *Maria*, the . . .-less[1] Virgin (παρθένος) . ., Apa *Moses*,[2] Apa *Shenoute*,[3] Apa *Pahôm* the Great,[4] Apa *Theôtór[os]*[5] . ., Apa *Pǵôl*,[6] Apa *Pshai*[7] . . ., holy (? ἅγιος) Apa *Sabinos*,[8] Apa *Petafios*,[9] Apa *Hôrouêse*,[10] Apa *Séte*(?), Apa *Papnoute*,[11] Apa *Magarios*,[12] Apa *Peléu*,[13] Apa (?) *Ouanlentinos*,[14] Apa *Thea*, Apa *Eihannês*,[15] Apa *Elisaios*, Apa *Hannisis*, Apa *O . . nesios*, Apa *Georgios*, Apa *Pêratos*(?), Apa *Mena*,[16] Apa *. a . pakêa*, Apa *[Sh]e[ne]tôm*,[17] Apa *Thêt* . . . ., Apa *Lebe[rios]*,[18] Apa *Biktor*,[19] Apa . . . *isas*, Apa *Gêros*,[20] Apa *Phibamôn*,[21] Apa *S[eu]éros*,[22] A[pa] . . .

The rest illegible. In the midst of the text, by a later hand: ' The lady (κυρά) *Panta* the little.'

48.—*Z*, S. Wall. Names: *Sousanna* (lower, *Tsousanna*), Apa *Nôch* (? Enoch[23]), ' . . . his father (?) ' Apa *Seprone* (? Sempronius, cf. B. 11, or Sophronius), ' my mother *Tarsene* (cf. Arsenius), Apa *Shenetom*, Apa *Oeumas* (? Thomas, Theudas[24]), ' the lady (κυρά) abbess ' (?? *apadêssa*), Apa *Paulos*.

33.—*Z*, S. Wall. Presumably names.

[1] 'Spotless' or the like.
Archimandrite of the local monastery (*v.* introductory §).
[3] The celebrated archimandrite of the White Monastery, ob. 451.
[4] For this form *v. Proc. Soc. Bibl. Arch.* xxi. 247.
[5] Pahôm's disciple and eventual successor.
[6] Shenoute's predecessor.
[7] Probably the Nitrian hermit, contemporary of Macarius.
[8] Here perhaps a break in the list, followed by local celebrities. For S. *v.* No. 16, or ? the bishop of Panopolis (*v.* Rossi, *Papiri* II, iii. 2).
[9] ? Patapios (*v.* Metaphrast, 8th Dec.).
[10] ? Read *Horsyése*, Pachôm's successor.
[11] There are several of this name.
[12] ? Macarius the Great.
[13] *Cf.* Crum, *Copt. Ostr.* No. 444.
[14] ? Valentinus, though the termination looks like *a* (fem.).
[15] Johannes (*cf.* Crum, *l.c.* p. xx).
[16] If not local, the celebrated military martyr of Alexandria.
[17] *Cf.* Crum, *l.c.* No. 105.
[18] ? The pope, ally of Athanasius and revered by Copts (*Synax.*, 9th Babeh).
[19] ? Martyr, son of Romanus.
[20] ? Cyrus (Abû Kîr).
[21] Military martyr (Amélineau, *Actes* 54).
[22] If this is correct, S. is probably the patriarch of Antioch, ob. 538.
[23] Or Noah (*Nôhe* in Saʿidic).
[24] Scarcely [Ap]a *Parsymas* (Barsoma).

37.—Chamber below Corr. of Kings, W. Wall. Apparently commemorative: ' I, *Tkalahône*[25] (fem.), this wretched one (ταλαίπωρος) . . .' In l. 3, σαββατον.

B. 12.—Prays ' the God of Michael ' on behalf of Apa *Kiros*(?), ' the wretched sinner, the deacon ' (*cf.* B. 11).

19.—*Z*, S. Wall. Names: Apa *Moses*, Apa *Sh[enoute]*, Ama *Sousanna*.

43.—Inner Court, S. Wall. Apparently names (? *Psotêr*) and disjointed phrases (*na nai παγαπη*).

41.—Chapel of Isis, N. Wall. Names: *Psôtêr*, others compounded with ' Isis ' (?).

49.—*Z*, S. Wall. Various names: ' . . . *Johannes* her son,' ' . . . *ora* the little, the novice ' (? *tbere*) ' Ama *Therebeke*.'[26]

35.—*Z*, E. Wall. On right: ' The prayer of the holy (ἅγιος) Apa *Basilios* ' (? the Great). On left: a name, Apa *Pe . . . ôphylos*.

40.—*Z*, N. Wall. 'Orans' and name: ' the lady (κυρά) *Panta* the little ' (*v.* No. 36).

21.—*Z*, S. Wall. Two names: *Tsophia* and *Mariham*.

34.—*Z*, W. Wall. Presumably names.

B. 3.—Commemorates Ama *Giorgia* ' the mother of us all,' Ama *Drosis* ' the mother of us all,' *Tanagnosta* (?) the little, adding a prayer for *Giorgia* and *Tashenoute* (?).

B. 4.—(collated by Miss Murray). Commemorates Ama *Giorgia*, the head,[27] Ama *Parthenope*, the major-domo (*trmnéi*). The former is in l. 11 called ' the mother of the monastery ' (*tmaau nthenete*). *Martha* the little and *A* . . . . the little, the teacher (*tsaχo*)[28] are also named; besides *Maria* (? the Virgin), Apa *Moses*, Apa *Shenoute* and Apa *Pahôm* the Great.

B. 11.—Begins: ' By God's will and the prayers of Apa *Moses* and Apa *Agathôn* ' . It relates to a woman, *Kelatheupente* (?)[29] whose sins (*ennesnobe*) God is prayed to forgive, and then enumerates the local ecclesiastical dignitaries: the deacon and steward (οἰκονόμος) [of the monastery ?] of *Tpouliané*,[30] the gardener (κωμαρίτης), the architect (*ekôt*[31]) archi-

[25] Names in *Kala-*, *v.* Crum, *l.c.* p. 67. Also Turaief, *Materiale po arch. christ.*, No. 29, *Pgalaîre*.
[26] = Rebecca (*Cf.* Crum, *Copt. Ostr.* p. 46) with fem. *t*.
[27] *V.* No. 11.
[28] This rare word happens to occur in the letters of Moses to this community of nuns (Zoega 531 = *Miss. franç.* iv. 696). *Cf. PSBA.* xxi. 249. Ll. 7, 8 read *ŝem tsaχo Maria Apa Môisês* &c.; 9. *Tomanna Drosis*.
[29] Can scarcely be correct ; but I am unable to amend it.
[30] = Bulianâ.
[31] *V.* Crum, *l.c.*, p. 41.

G

mandrite, teacher (? *sah* l. 9). Then it is said that Apa *Petronius*, presumably the abbot, had died that year and set Apa *Theodorus* in his place ; *David* being bishop [1] and *Gabriel* archbishop [at the time]. From these last words a date for this graffito can be suggested ; for it may be presumed that the Gabriel named is the patriarch of A.D. 910—21, not G. ibn Tarik of the 12th century.

42.—Outer Court, pillar A. Begins: 'By the will of God and the prayers of the Saints,' and commemorates the rise of the water to a certain point,[2] in the month of Mesore. Ll. 5—8, prayer to God ' the pitiful, the compassionate' (*pnaêt pšanhtêf*) on behalf of 'Apa *Georgios*(?) my brother' and others. *Cf.* Nos. 13, 22, 38, 44, 47, and B. 13, 15, 17, whence the gaps here may be filled.

13.—Outer Court, pillar A. Beginning of a text similar to No. 42 ('By the will of God' &c.). Written upon incised hieroglyphics.

6.—*Z*, N. Wall. Begins : ' By the will of God and the prayers of the saints' (*cf.* Nos. 13, 42). Asks for mercy (*ouna*) and blessing (*ekasmou*) on a woman (*eros*).

44.—Corridor of Kings (= B. 18). A Thanksgiving for the adequate (?) rise of the Nile (*cf.* Nos. 42 &c.). ' We thank thee, Lord God, Almighty (παντοκρ.), that thou hast had pity upon our poverty and hast had pity upon thy creature (πλάσμα) which thou didst form and hast showed forth thy power among the people (λαός) and shut (= *štam*) the mouth of the Sadducees and hast brought the water up for us to the *hame*(?), on the 25th of Mesourê, the day of Apa *Moses*. I(?) bless thee, Father, I bless thee, Son, I bless thee, Holy Ghost. We(?) heartily (*tónou*) give thee thanks (εὐχαριστεῖν), that thou hast given us means, this heavy (*ethêš*) year, to . . ' There are faint traces of 2 ll. below those copied.

38.—Pillar in Chamber beyond Corr. of Kings (partly = B. 14). The first 7½ ll. seem to be commemorative : '. . . . . wretched (ταλαίπωρος), who is full of sickness and grief and groans (*hilupê hiašahom*) ; she obtained her rest (? *enasjï nnesmton*) in her youth ' (? ? *hn . . mntkoui*). The rest is effaced by a later text, relating to the rise of the Nile (*cf.* Nos. 42 &c.). ' By the will of God and the prayers of the saints, [the] wat[er] rose [to] the *hame* [on the] 25th of Me[so]rê, our . . . being at An-

tinoe (*Antinóou*). Afterwards, in (?) another year on the 19th Mêsorê, (being?) two years after one another.' The last lines record that something was done ' on Saturday.'

47.—Chamber behind Corr. of Kings, little wall, back. Relates to the rise of the water (*cf.* No. 42 &c.) to the *hame*, on the 29th of Mesôrê, ' while I, *Maria* the little, did the weekly duty ' (*r-ėβδομας*).[3]

B. 13.—Records the water's rise, as in No. 42 &c., on the 26th Mesore ' of the year when our holy father, Apa *Pesynthius* departed (? ἀποδημεῖν) and came to us.[4] May his holy blessing come in love (ἀγάπη) upon us.' Then : ' I, *Ana* (?) was scribe (ἀπογράφειν) ; I recorded (*lit.* wrote) the water ' . . . . . If this refers to Pesynthius, the well-known bishop of Coptos, it should be dated about A.D. 620.

B. 15.—Records the water's rise, as in 42 &c., on the 28th of Mesore, when *Hellaria* did the weekly service (*v.* No. 47, B. 16). Then an obscure reference to στοά and στῦλος with the names of the archimandrite and of *Tsousanna*, 'his daughter,' the major-domo (*rmenêi*).

B. 17.—' By the will of God and the prayers of the archangels Michael and Gabriel and of the holy Virgin ' . . ., [the water rose] to the *hame* on the 29th of Mesore, ' on the day of our Lord Jesus Christ.—I bless thee, Father' (&c., as in No. 3). Ll. 15 ff. appear to refer to someone (a woman) who is ill and to invoke *Cyrus, Colluthus* and *Cosmas* and *Damianus*,[5] ' the physicians, healers ' (*nrefrpahre etetnarpahre*). She who ' recorded the water ' for the year also gives her name (illegible).

B. 16.[6]—' Blessed be the Lord (εὐλογητός κύριος). I, *Maria* the little, the Ethiopian, did (*lit.* do) the weekly service[7] on the birth-day of the great lady[8] (*i.e.* abbess). I did clean (*ti-καθαρον*), I gathered (?)[9] the honey, I . . . (*lit.* gave) the . . .[10] for taking the dates. May the Lord bless her and her sister *Lydia* and her(?) father and their brother *Moses* ' (?). The final words are in a cryptogram which I can not solve.

---

[2] *Cf.* B. 15, 16 and Ladeuze, *Pachome*, 296.
[4] ' After having come to us ' scarcely allowed by grammar.
[5] Celebrated medical saints : 1. ' Ahû Kîr,' colleague of John at Alexandria ; 2. Pysician, martyred at Antinoe ; 3, 4. Syrian physicians and martyrs.
[6] I have here been able to use a tracing made by Mr. H. L. Christie.
[7] *V.* No. 47.
[8] *V.* Crum, *Copt. Ostr.* p. 53.
[9] *Lit.* gave or sold.
[10] *Kalyllion*, cf. ? *kallóre* (Zoega 506), some agricultural tool.

---

[1] Buliná was probably in the diocese of Diospolis (Hou).
[2] The word *hame* (? = *home*) is obscure and apparently unknown except in these texts.

22.—Chamber below Corr. of Kings, W. Wall. Partly in cryptogram, not however on the system ($\theta = a$, $\eta. = \beta$ &c.) usual with the Copts (*cf.* B. 16). Ll. 5, 6 relate to the rise of the water, perhaps in the month Thoth (*cf.* No. 42 &c.). Possibly two texts here confused.

17.—Outer Court, pillar D. End (?) of a text : . . *etnéu ebol.*

15.—Outer Court, pillar D. An obscure text.

45.—*Z*, W. Wall. Obscure.

46.—*Z*, E. Wall. Obscure.

Two Stelae (Pl. XXXVII).—Brought from Abydos, 1901; now in the Fitzwilliam Museum, Cambridge. The text of the larger (marble), after invoking the Trinity, states that 'in this place' the body ($\sigma\kappa\dot\eta\nu\omega\mu\alpha$) lies[1] of the deceased Apa *Theodóros*, of blessed (*lit.* good) memory, son of the deceased *Moses*, presbyter, of *Tpolybiané*[2] (= Belyanâ), who went to rest on the 2d of Phamenôth, in the year of Diocletian 655 (= A.D. 939). 'May God rest his soul and lay him in the bosom of Abraam and Isaac and Jacob and make him worthy to hear the merciful and compassionate voice (saying :) Come ye blessed' (&c., Mt. xxv, 34).

The smaller stele (limestone) invokes [the Trinity, Virgin] Prophets, Apostles and all saints and com-memorates Paul, who died on the 29th of Paone, in the 10th Indiction.

Wine Jar. (Pl. XXXVII).—Texts from an earthenware pitcher, 2 ft. 2 in. high, found in 1901. Written in four parallel columns. Its heading is : 'The account ($\lambda\acute{o}\gamma o\varsigma$) of the wine (*pl.*) which we sold (*or* gave) at the vintage ($\kappa\alpha\rho\pi\acute{o}\varsigma$) of the ? Indiction' (*sop*).[3] This is followed by a list of names, generally in pairs, with the amounts of wine opposite them. Among the names may be noted :—Col. 1, *Pephan* = Epiphanius; *Charif* cf. Chêrêp, Cairo 8377; *Paoua* cf. col. 4 *Paou*; *Pitou*, $\Pi\acute{\iota}\tau o\upsilon\varsigma$; *Palots* cf. $\Pi\alpha\lambda\omega\tau\acute{\iota}\varsigma$.

Ostracon (pottery) (Pl. XXXVII).—'Before my words, I greet my beloved father, in all the fullness of my soul ($\psi\upsilon\chi\acute{\eta}$), and (also) *Tachêl*. Thou didst speak with me concerning the holy church; I took courage ($\theta\alpha\rho\rho\epsilon\hat\iota\nu$) and prayed with the men. As for the tremision-(worth) of bricks, I know that thou dost never change (? thy mind) at all, especially ($\mu\acute{\alpha}\lambda\iota\sigma\tau\alpha$) in the affairs of God. Lo, I have sent a hundred[4] bricks. Now if thou wilt have patience[5] as to the other hundred, that (*sic*) the Lord may watch over you (*sic*) for a long time.[6]

'Give it to my teacher *Johannes*, from *Pahômô* the priest ($\pi\rho\epsilon\sigma\beta\acute{\upsilon}\tau\epsilon\rho o\varsigma$), his humble ($\dot\epsilon\lambda\acute{\alpha}\chi\iota\sigma\tau o\varsigma$) scholar.'[7]

W. E. CRUM.

---

[1] A very rare formula. Recurs, stele Alexandria Museum, No. 296.

[2] Apparently the original form of *Tbulsané* (*Aeg. Z.* '78. 26) and *Tpourané.* Prof. Petrie suggests 'the Lybian town,' indicating a settlement in Greek times.

[3] *Cf. Mitth. Rainer* I. 17. But the reading is uncertain. Perhaps $\kappa\alpha\tau\grave{\alpha}$ $\pi\rho\acute{o}\sigma\omega\pi o\nu.$

[4] *3e n-* repeated by mistake.

[5] Reading $\dot{\alpha}\nu\acute{\epsilon}\chi\epsilon\iota\nu.$

[6] Reading *oueii* = *ouoeii.* But the sentence is obscure and its construction faulty.

[7] Reading *sboui.*

INDEX.

LONDON
PRINTED BY GILBERT AND RIVINGTON, LTD.,
ST. JOHN'S HOUSE, CLERKENWELL, E.C.

1. VIEW LOOKING SOUTH, SHOWING
DIRECTION OF TRENCH.

2. DOORWAY OF SCULPTURED CHAMBER, LOOKING NORTH.

3. VIEW OF GREAT HALL, S. AND W. WALLS.

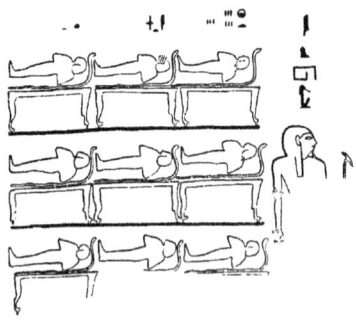

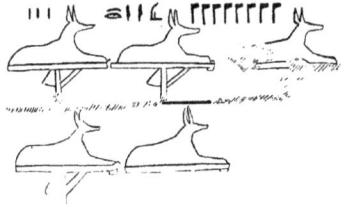

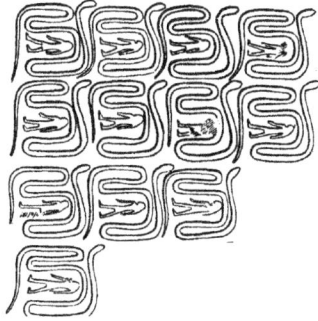

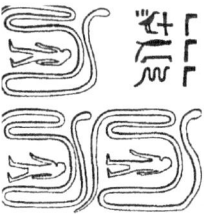

SOUTH WALL

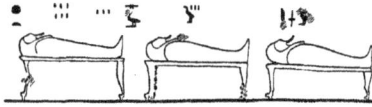

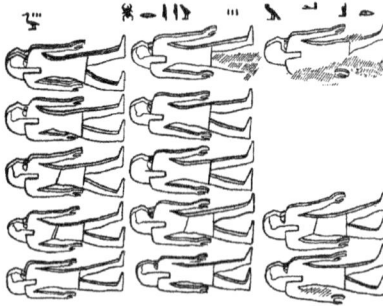

WEST WALL

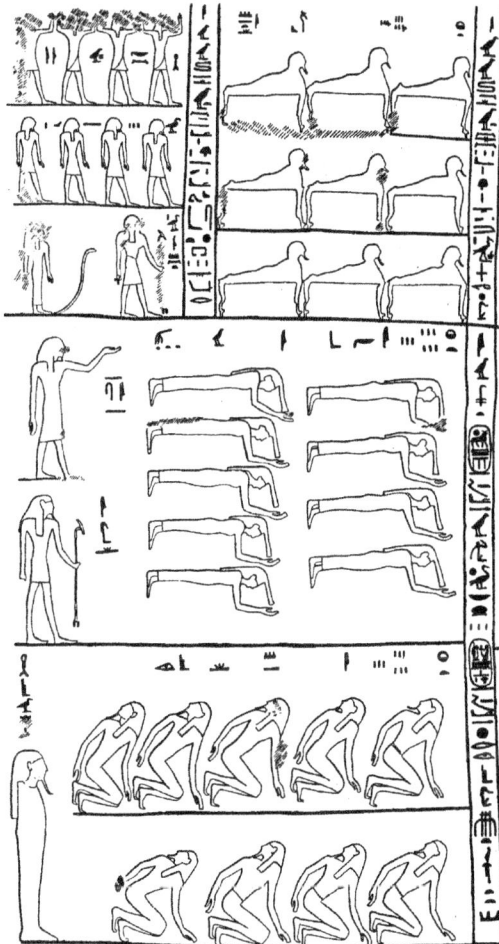

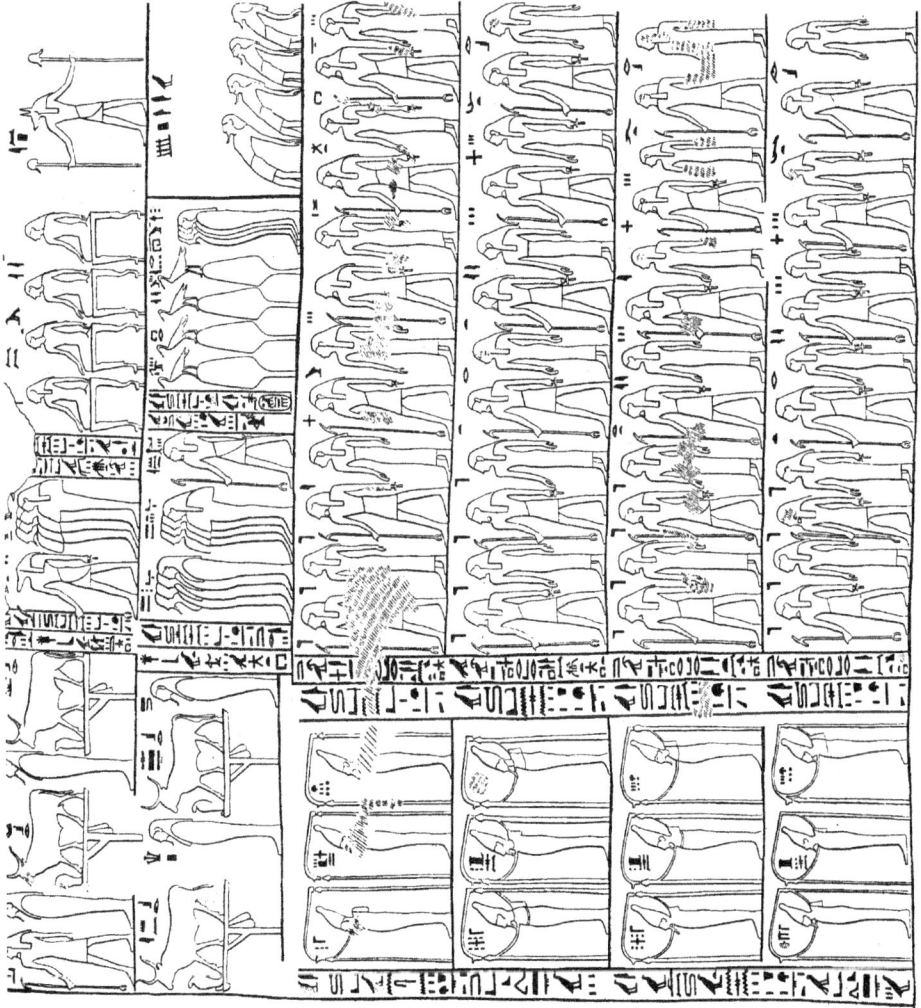

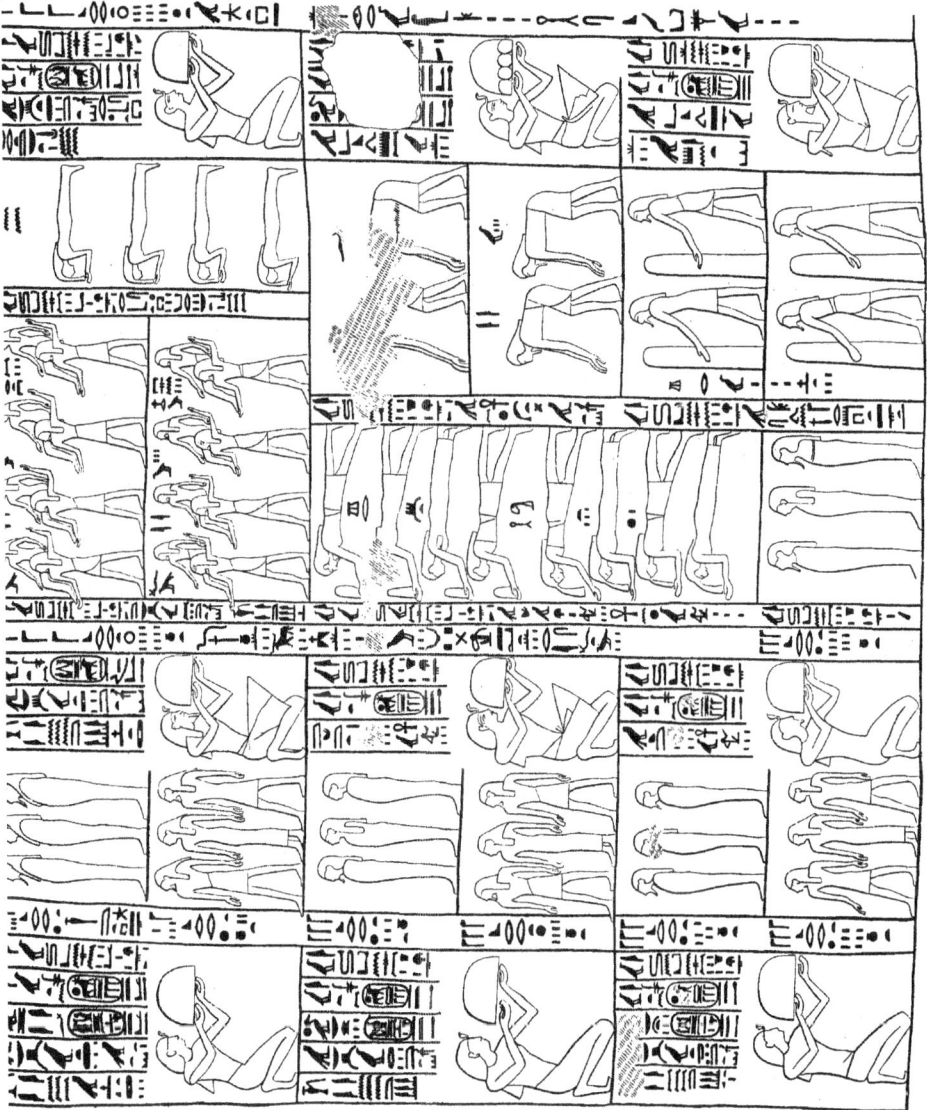

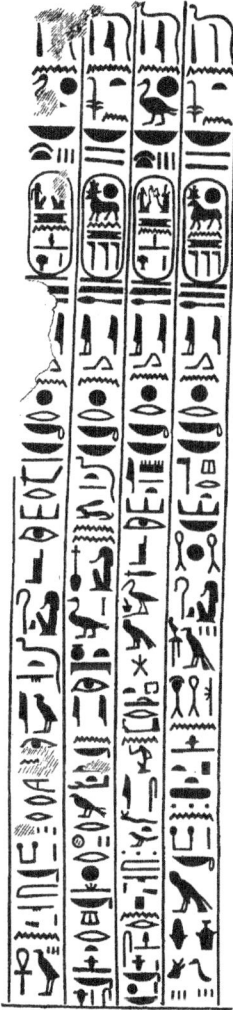

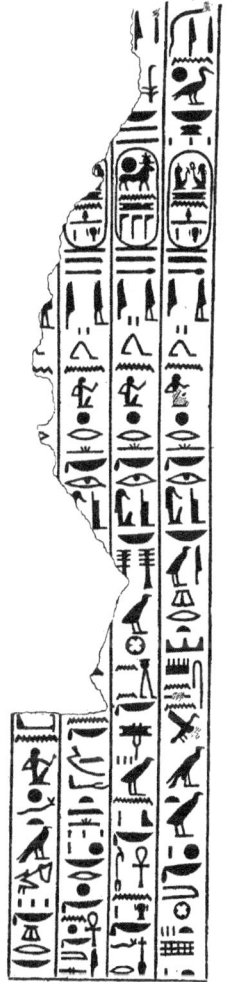

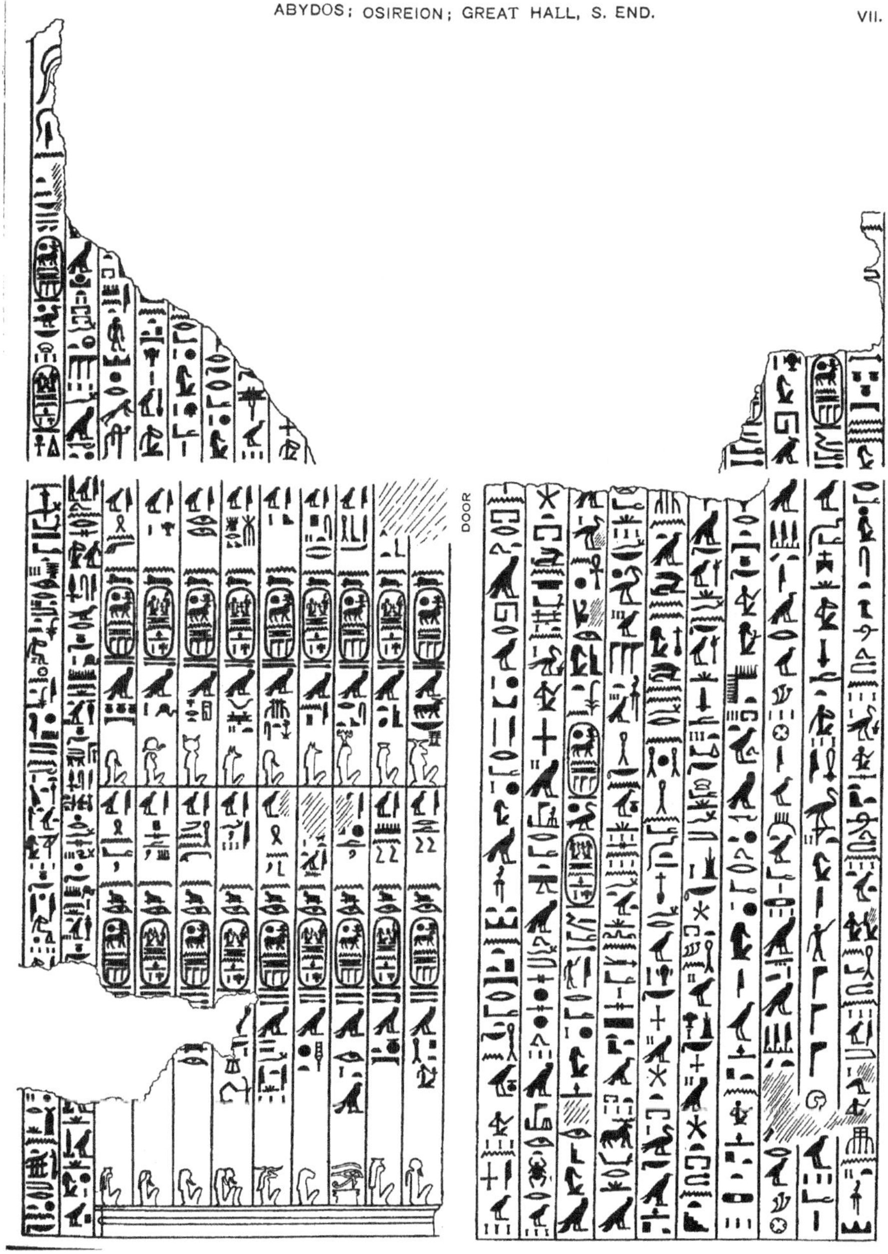
DOOR

ABYDOS, OSIREION, HALL, WEST WALL, MID.   IX

ABYDOS, OSIREION, HALL, WEST WALL, N. END.

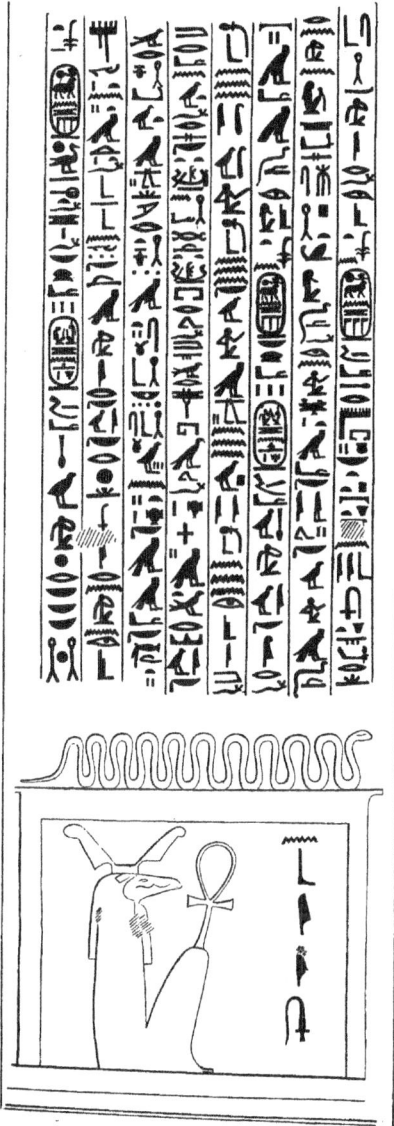

DOORWAY

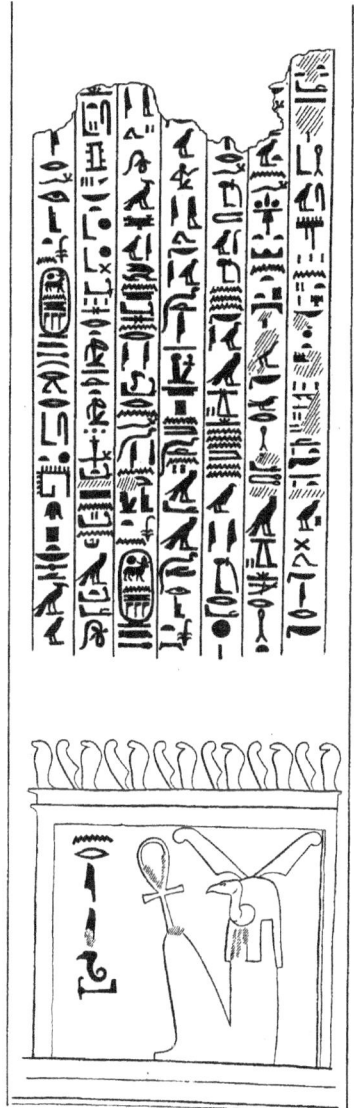

M.A.M.

3 10 IN HALL

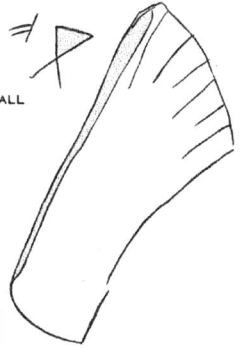

N. WALL

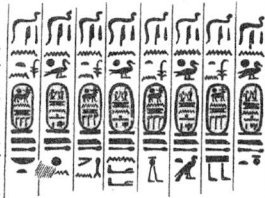

S. WALL

LINTEL

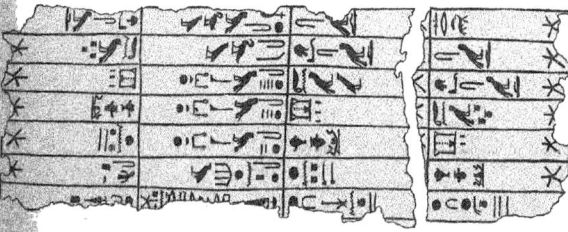

H.P.
M.A.M.

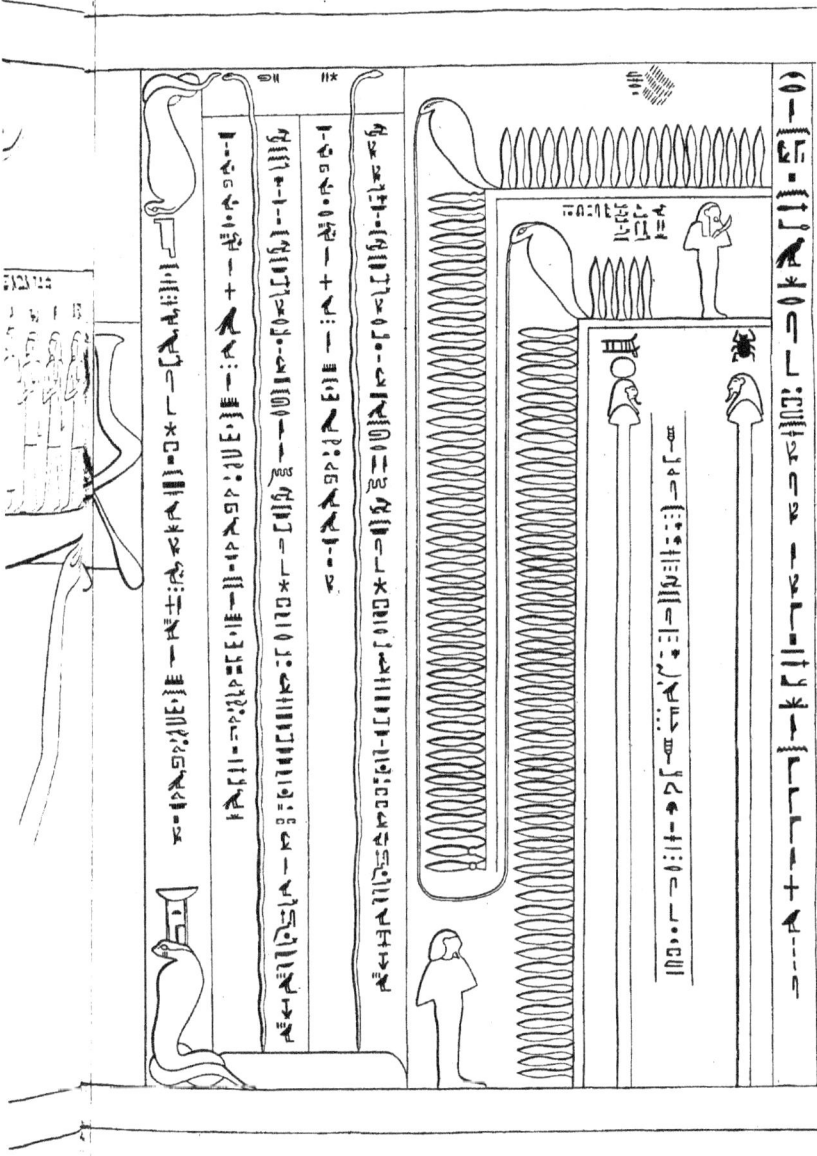

F.H.
M.A.M.

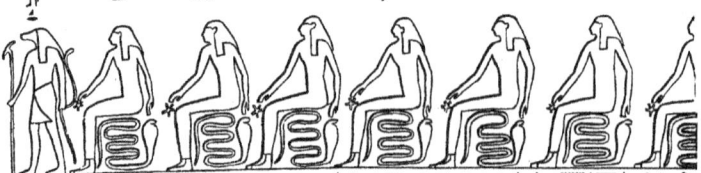

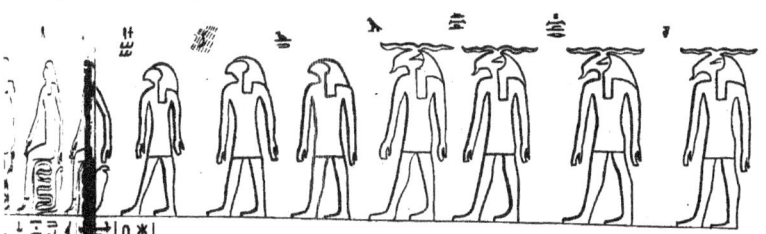

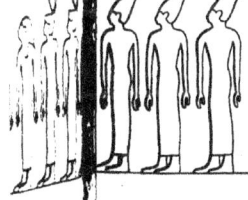

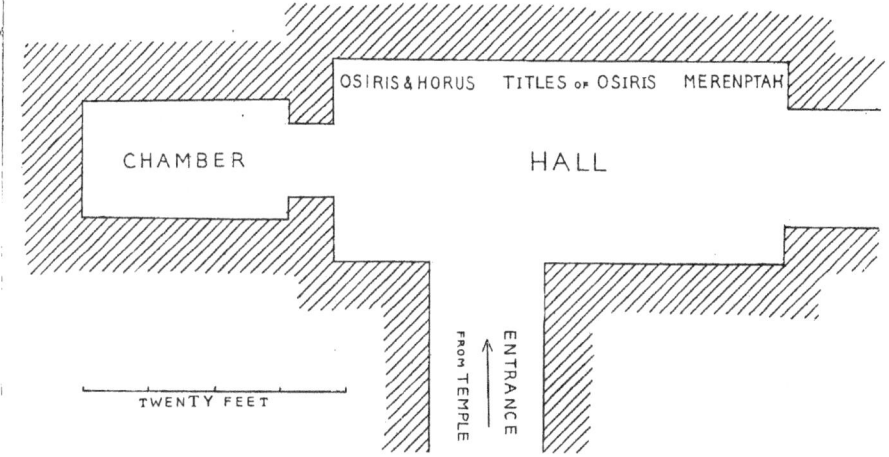

OSIRIS & HORUS   TITLES of OSIRIS   MERENPTAH

CHAMBER

HALL

ENTRANCE FROM TEMPLE

TWENTY FEET

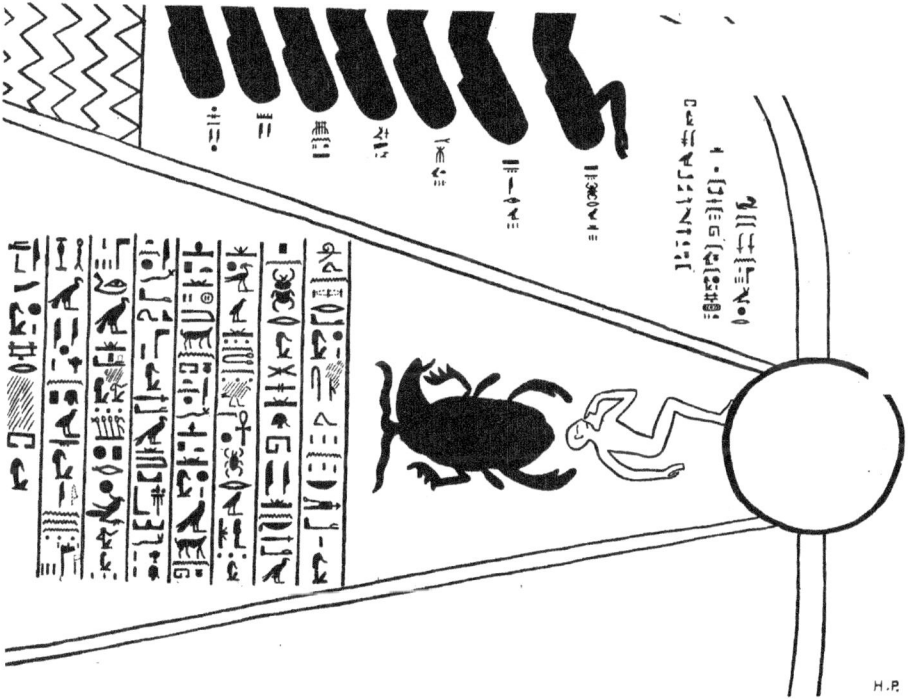

H.P.
M.A.M.

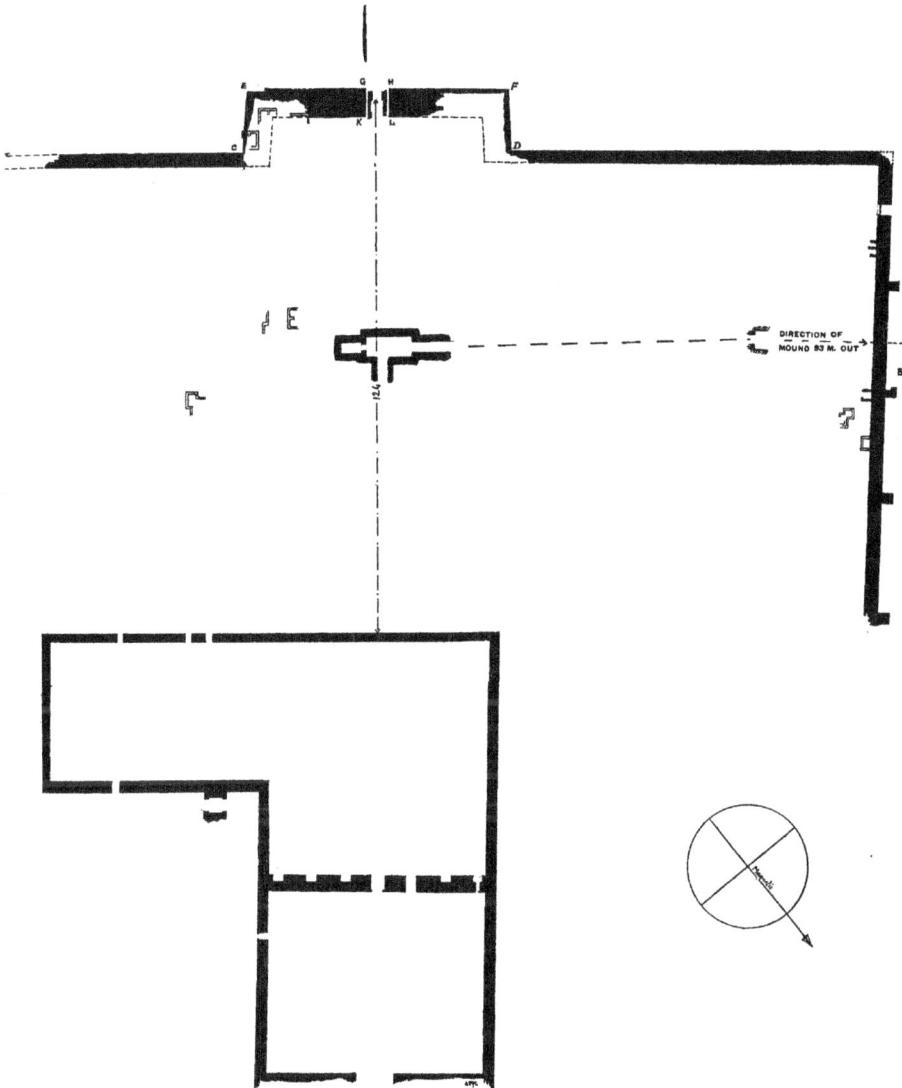

DIRECTION OF
MOUND 83 M. OUT

1. OSIRIS ENCIRCLING THE DUAT.

2. HEAD. OF MERENPTAH.

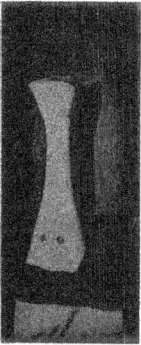

3. POTTERY STAND.

4. SCULPTOR'S TRIAL PIECES. 5.

6. PLASTER CASTS.

7. SURVEYOR'S MARK.—ROMAN.

F.L.G.

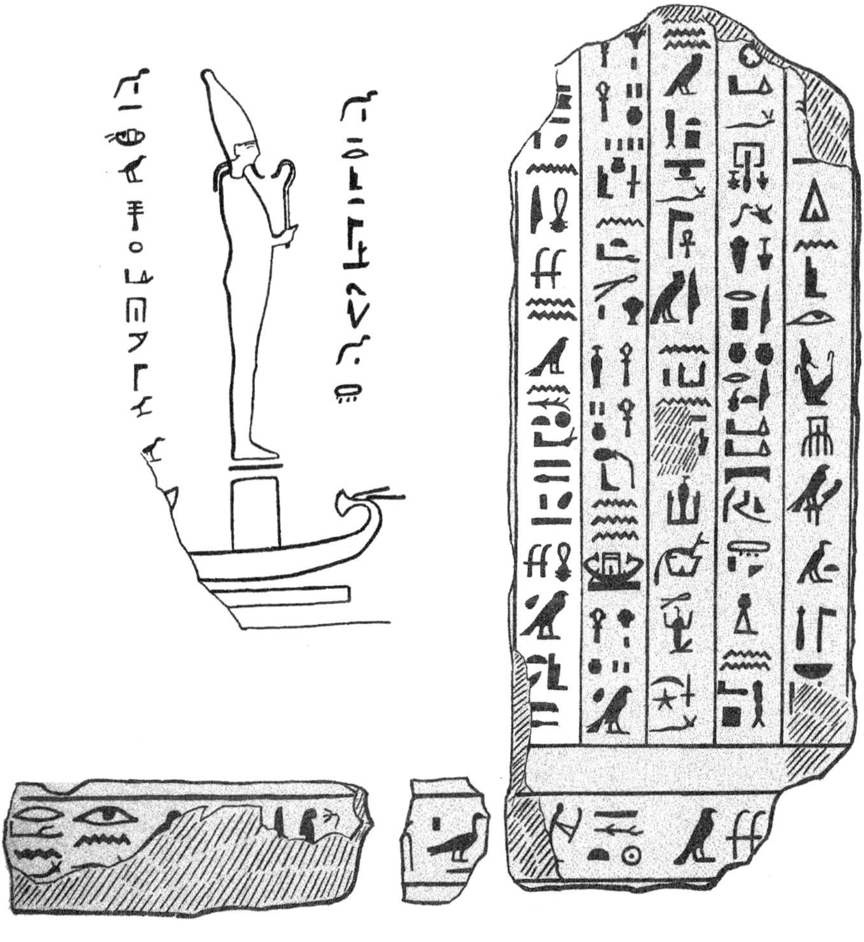

M.A.M.

APICTIC
ATIKETO
TIMAP
XOC
N OTIOC
APOMWN

ΕΠΙΦΑΤΗC
ΝΙΚΙΜΩ

ωΗΜΕΧΙ ΗΡΑΚΛΕΙΤΟCΠΟΛΕΜΑΡΧ
ΑΧΑΙΟCΑΦΙΚΕΤΟ

ΓCωΙΙωΙΝΠΛΟΥΤΟ ΓΕΝΩΥ

ΑΤ ΟΜCωΤΟCΠΤΟΛΕΜΑΙΟΥ

ΑΡΙCΤΟΚΛΗC

ΤΥΠΛΚΥΝΗΑΤΤΟΜΕΝΩ

L.E.
M.A.M.

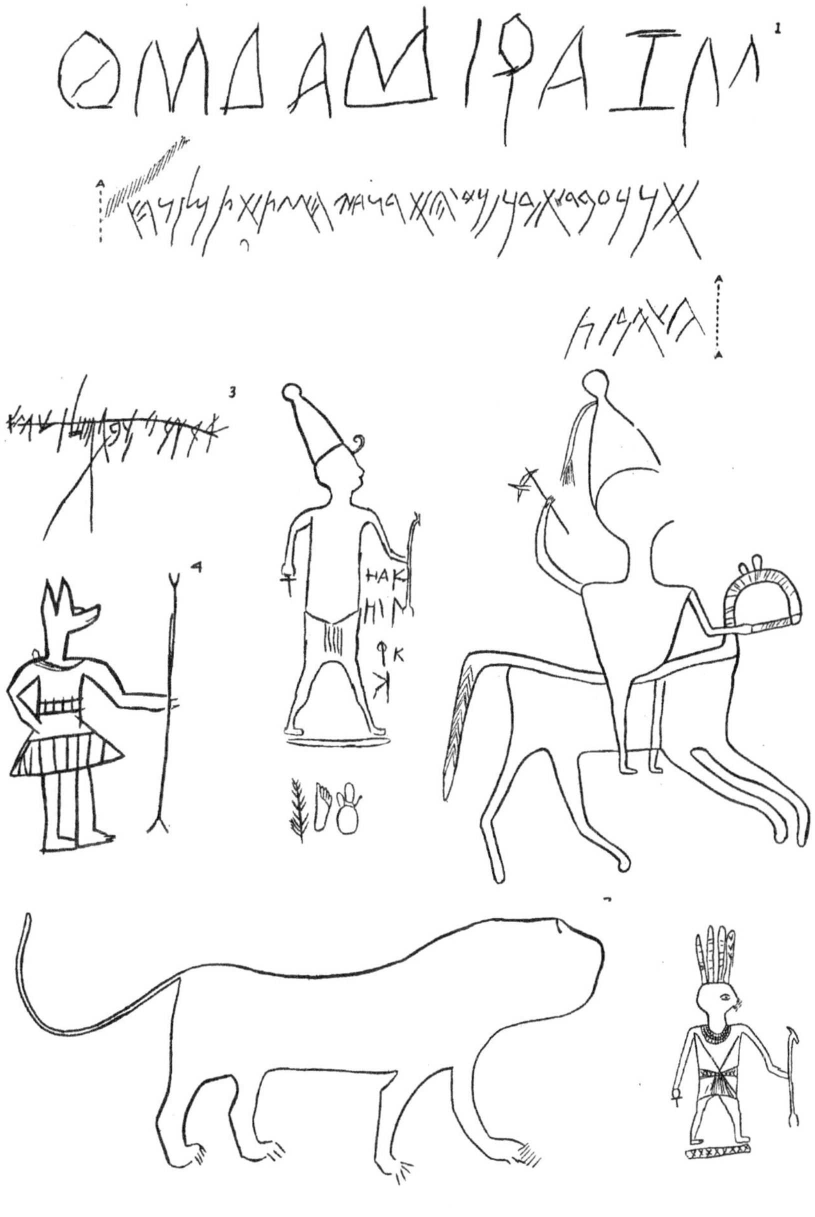

ΥF

ΥΤΡΟΝ

ΓΘΠΡΝΗΚΥ3ΗΙΜΙ
ΕΔΙΣΘΜΟΥΜΔΡΔΗΥ

ΥΜΕΗΣΟΙΝ

ΖΔΖΕΛΜΙΥ ΣΚΕΙΞ

ΑΡΤΕΜΙΔΩΡΟSΗΚΚΩΕΠΙΣΙ— ΔΞ

ΗΝΔΓΟΡΔΣΖΩΜΘΥΠΚΦΟΣΙΚΩΕΥΟΥΕΚΚΤ

ΤΔΛΘΤΤΡΙΟΙ

ΑΗΘΥΦΕΥΣΗΚΥ

Η

ΥΗ

ΘΝΗΤΟΣΔΤΤΙΝΟΥΘΕΙΣΛΝΣΗΚΩ

ΤΟΠΡΟΚΥΝΗΜΔΔΗΛΗΤΡΙΟΥΤΙ 9

ΦΙΛΟΚΡ ΧΤΙΙΣ

10

ΛΕΑΓΙ

ΠΤ ΥΗ ΤΙΝ
ΟΚΛΙΣΣΕΟΥΕΤΙΠΡΟΣΚΥΝΩΝΧΔΙΡΕΙΝΛΕΓΩ

ΦΙΛΟΚΛΗΣ ΙΕΡΟΚΛΕΟΥΣΤΡΟΙΣΚΝΙΟΣ ΠΔΡΕΓΕΝΙΣΔΚΗΤΡΟΣΚΥΝΩΝΤΟΝΣΔΡΔ
ΙΝ ΤΙΝ

ΕΠΙΓΙΙΣΛΡΥΦΟΥΠΟΧΙΟΡΚΙΔΣΣΕΠΔΗΝΙΚΗ

13

ΤΟΠΡΟΣΚΥΝΗΜΔΗΡΔΚΛΗ...ΝΙΟΝ...
ΤΟΠΡΟΣΚΥΝΗΜΔΔΗΜΗΤΡΙΟΥΤΚΝΔΤΟΧ...ΚΔΙΠΟΤΟΜΩΝΟΣΠΔΤΤΟΣΚΔΔΗΜΗΤΡΙΟΥΛΔΕΩ

L.E.

ΚΑΠωΝΟΣΚΑΙΔΗΜΑΤΡΟΣ [14] ΘΓΟΦΙΛΟ ΣΑΤΡΟΣ [15]
ΤΟΠΡΟϹΚΥΝΗΜΑΩΔΕ

ΨΜΟϹΤΒΥΚΗϹ

ΝΙ [16]   ΗΙΛΚΛΗΣ [17]   ΛΗΤΟΔΛΡΙΟϹ [18]
ΑΛ   ϹΟΝΑΒΙΝΘΘΕΟϹ
ϪΛ   Ιϲ
                      ΤΑ   ΛΡΙϹ
ΑΡΝ
                             ΤΑΓΗϹ
ΜΕΝΕΚΡΑΤΕΙΡΤΥΚΕΙΝ   ΠΑΜΝΑϹ
                      Ν.ΑΑΡΑΥϹϹΠΕΤ

ΠΑΡΑΓΕΓΟΝΕΝΑΓΑΘΕΝΟΘΙΔΕωΤΤ [19]
ΙΙΑΙΠΑΡΕΓΕΤΟΔΕΚΑΙΔΙΕΜ ΗΤΙΙ
ωΠΑΡωΝΥΜΙϽΝΙΛΛϹΚΛΟΝΥϹΙΚΙ
ΙΟΥΡΑΤΗΠΧΑΡϹΕΟΤΡΑΤΗϹΥΝΠΑΙϹ
ΤΟΠΙΚΙΚΗΜΥΡΙωΚΑΝΙΟϹΠΕΠΓΙϹ

                              ΛΥΘΘΟϟΥ [21]
ΑΝΛΟΥΘΙΗΙϹ   ϳΧΜΥΡϽ [20]   ΤΟΠΡΟΗΚωΙϹΑΡΑΙ
ΧΥϹΙΤΗϹ   ΔΙΟΝΥϹΙΟϹ
                           ΑΜΙΧΑΡΟΥϹ
                           ϟϟϟϥϝΙ
ΚΛ ΨΛΥΨ ϟΙΗΤΗ [22]   ΑΠϹΤΓΛΨΗΜΙΑ 1996
ϟϽϪϲϞΠ   Δ   ΝΑϹΗΚω
                              ΔΘΝΜΕΤΑ
ΛϮΛΟΥΘΙΗΚΛ   ΤΠΟΥ
                          _ϳΤΕϟΡΒΕϞΧΙΝ
                           ΠΛΤΟΥΤΟϹΚΛΛΚ
                           ΚϜΙΤΟϞΡΛΕΑΦΟ
                              ΑΜΝΑΚ ΥϹ
                              ΕϞΙΝΙϹ
                              ΤΟΚΟΙΟΙϹ

ΝΕΟΠΤΟΛΕ.ΜΟϹΜ ΡϽΥΚΛϹΕΠϽϲΙ Ϟ [23]
          ΠΥΘΟΔωΡϹϹ

ΠϪⲰⲘⲉⲚⲉⲘⲠⲉϫⲠⲟⲚⲉⲓⲧⲠⲉⲩⲥⲠϣⲏⲣⲉⲚⲟⲁⲭⲉⲓⲠⲠϣⲏⲣⲉⲚⲚⲃ

ⲉⲡⲓⲧⲉⲡⲉⲣⲉϫⲁϫ ϫⲓⲧⲱⲧⲟⲕⲉϫⲥⲁⲓⲚⲚϣⲁⲭⲉⲉⲧⲃⲉⲚⲉϩⲃⲚⲉ ⲩⲧⲱⲧⲚϩⲧϫⲣⲁⲓⲚϩⲏⲧⲟⲩ

ⲦⲱⲢⲬⲎⲘⲠⲉⲟⲩⲁⲅⲅⲉⲗⲓⲟⲛ ⲚⲦⲤ Ⲡⲉ

ⲚⲦⲁⲩⲍⲱⲟⲕⲟⲛⲚⲦⲉⲣⲉⲩⲉⲓⲉⲃⲟⲗ ⲁ ⲕⲧⲁϣⲉⲩ

ⲁ ⲁⲚⲠⲉⲓⲱⲚ ϥⲙⲟⲩⲁϥⲕⲱⲧ ⲟⲩⲁⲃ ϊⲭⲏⲙⲉⲚⲟⲩ

ⲱⲠⲉⲇⲉϩⲚⲠⲧⲣⲉⲩⲥⲙ ⲟⲕⲉⲣⲟⲟⲕⲁⲩⲟⲕⲉⲙⲙⲟⲟⲕⲁⲁⲃ ⲕ ⲁ

ⲚⲁⲧⲁⲕⲱⲧⲱⲦⲟⲕⲉⲭⲚⲚⲚⲉⲦϣⲱ

ⲕⲉⲩⲧⲁⲩⲣⲟⲙⲠⲩⲓⲭⲉⲙⲚⲙⲁⲉⲓ ϣⲩ

ⲚⲦⲉⲉⲠⲓⲥⲧⲱⲗⲏϩⲚⲦⲁⲅϊⲭⲙ Ⲛⲉⲙ

ⲱⲱ ⲠⲙⲇⲉⲧⲟⲩⲚⲁⲧⲁ ⲉ ⲟⲁⲚ

ⲚⲦⲉϑϊⲭⲚⲥϩⲁⲓⲚ ⲉ

ⲚⲦⲉⲙⲁⲚⲦⲓⲕⲉⲓϫ

ⲚⲚⲢⲕⲉⲓϣⲠⲠⲚⲟ

Ⲛⲩϣⲉϩⲁⲙⲉ

ⲉⲦⲉⲚⲙⲙⲱ

ⲚϩϩⲚⲱⲚⲉϩ

ϩⲁⲙⲏⲚ

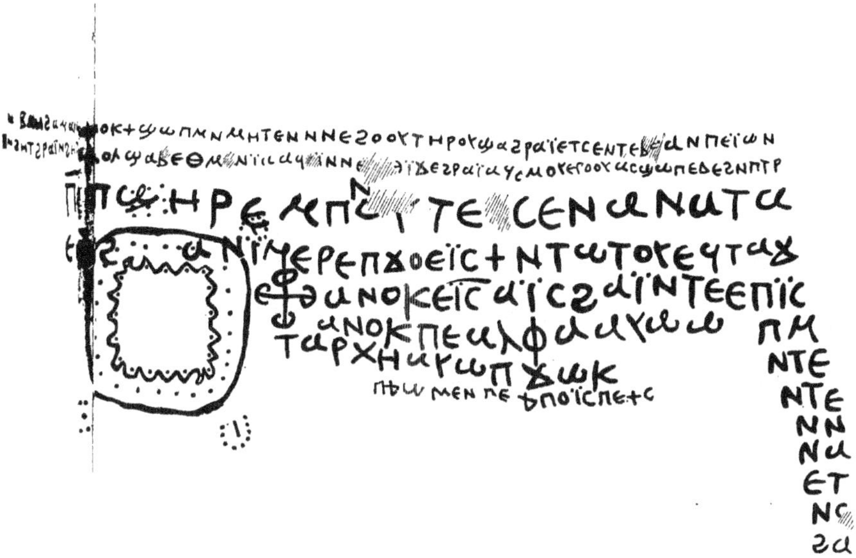

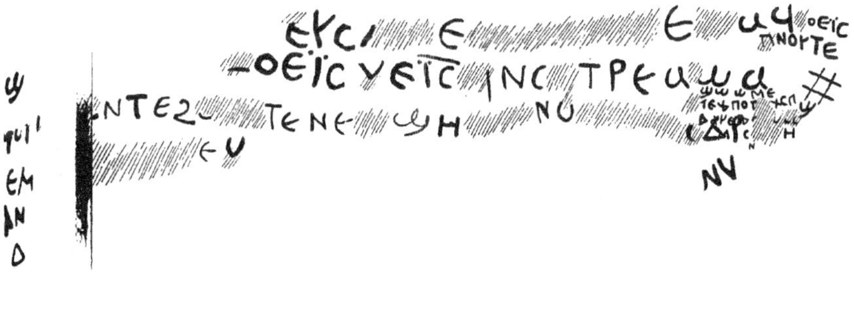

ΗΔΙ · · ο ΝαΠ сΤΟΛΟС Π

ΠΕΤΟΥΜΟΥΤΕ ΕΡΟ ΨΧΕΠΕΤΡ

ΕΙΑΚΟΒΟС ΠΩΗΡΕΝ ξΕΒΕΔΗΟС Π

ΠΧΟΟΜ Π ΠΕΧΠΟ Ιс ΠΕΧ Π

ΠΩΗΡΕΝΑ ΒΡΑΖΑΝ ΑΤΩΕΙС ΖΗΗΤ

ΗΡΟΥ ωος ΖΡΑΙΑΤ ΝΤΕΛΙΑΝ Π

ΤΑΜΑΝΝΕ

ΤΑΜΝΝΕΙ

ΤΕΑΡ α

ΧΡΝ

ⲘⲀⲢⲐⲆ 2
ⲰⲘ

ⲠⲠⲈ
ⲚⲌ ⲓⲥⲧⲉⲩ
ⲐⲀⲚⲚⲎⲥⲡ ⲩⲥⲟⲗ
ⲧⲁⲩⲉⲓⲧ ⲩⲗⲏⲧⲛⲛⲛⲉϩⲟⲟⲩ ⲏⲢ ᴬ
ⲕ✝ⲱⲟ
ⲧⲥ
ⲭⲢ

ЄΡΟΚ Π
✝ϩΥ ϹΜΟΥ ЄΡΟΚ ЄΙѠΤ ✝ϹΜΟΥЄΡ ϹΚ ΠΥΗ
✝ϹΜ ЄΡΟΚ ЄΠΠ ЄΤΟ ΚΑΒ ✝✝ ЄѠΟΝ
ΑΥ Ѡ ΚΥΡΙϹΤΑΝΑΚΙЄ ΤЄΙѠΑ
ΙΡ Α ЄΛѠЄΙϹΑΒΑѠΘ ΠΠ ΝΤѠΚ
Η ΤΜ ΟϹ ΝΤΠЄ ΠΚ ΑϨ ΠЄΤЄ
ΠЄΤ ϹΑϨΡΑΪΑΧ ϨΡΜ ΝΝ ΝЄ
ЄΡЄ ЄΙΑΦΙΝ Ρ ЄΝΝЄ ΙΤΝϨ
ΠЄΙ ΡЄϨЄΝ ѠΝ Є ѠΝ
ΖΙ ЄΟΥϹΙΑ ϨΤЄΟΜϨ ΙΘΡΙΝΟϹ ϨΙ
ΜΠЄΥΚΡΑΤΟϹ ЄΥ ΠΡΟϹΚΥΝЄΙΝΤ
ЄΥϹΜΟΥ ΑΡΟΥ ΜΝ ΠЄΥΜЄΡΙΤ ΝΟΥЄΤΟΥΑ
ΠЄΝϪΟЄΙϹ ΜΝ ΠЄΥ Π ΠΑЄΤΟΥΑ
ЄϨΝΚΑΡѠΟΙ ϪЄ ΑΓΙΟϹ Α
ΤΠЄΜΠ ΠΚΑϨ ΜЄϨ ЄΒΟΛ ϨΜ ΠЄ
✝ΤϪѠ ΜΜΟΚ ΠϪΟЄΙϹ Π ΝΟΥΤ
ΠЄΙ ΠЄΝϪΟЄΙϹ ΙϹ ΠЄΧϹ
Π ΟΓЄΝΗ
ΙѠΤ

ρскпγ·
вттеωω
ειωα
    ΝΤωρ

ΠΕ...ωοπq
Νͷ...ΒΙΝ
ͷΜΕΙΤΝ...ειωμπεͷ...ϊοοκ γΓΕΙΟϹ
...ραΓΓειος...ιαͷ
...χοΕΙϹϹΥΠΟϊ

ΥΝΕΙΝε̄οογΕΤΟͷαα
ΜΕΡΙΤε̄
ΕΤΟΥΔ·ΕΙϹΧϹ
ϲαϊοωͷ...Βοͷθ
ͷΗΠΕͷͷϹΕαΡͷͷ
ΠΝΟΥΓΕΤΟͷαͷΒ
ΕΧΙ...τω
ΓΕͷ
ιωϊ
        Р

...ΥωͷΕΝΠΝΟΥΓΕ
...ΛΗ ΝΕΤΟΥΔΟ
...ΚΝΑ
...ΜΕ
ΕΚα ΠΟΥΕΡΟϹ

⳨ θΕΟΥΧαΡΙϹ
  ͷΗΜ

Πͷ...ΠΝΟΥΓΕΠϹωΤΗΡ
ΝαΓαθΟϹΕΚαΡΟΕΙϹΡΟΝ
ΠΕͷΟΟΥΝΙΜ

Π ΧΟΕΙϹ
ΠΝΟΥΤΕ
ΙϹΧϹΚ ΥΡα

ΤϹΟΑΙϹΔ...ΗΤ

M. A M.

ι ⲍⲙⲡⲉⲙⲙⲱⲛⲁⲡ
ⲁⲣⲅⲉⲛⲟⲥⲙⲛⲛⲥⲟⲡⲥⲙⲡⲟⲩⲭⲁⲁⲅⲓ ⲟⲥⲁ
ⲃⲧⲛⲧⲉⲕⲝⲓⲭⲁⲍⲣⲁⲓⲛⲕⲉⲕⲟⲩ
ⲟ ⲙⲉⲙⲛ ⲧⲣⲛⲟⲟⲩⲱⲛⲍⲛⲥⲛⲟⲩⲁ
ⲡ ⲏⲧⲉⲛⲁⲍⲣⲁⲓⲛⲍⲏⲧⲟⲡⲉⲧⲍ ⲕⲁⲓ
ⲥⲉⲣⲁⲫⲉⲓⲛ ⲍⲣⲡⲧⲓⲕⲉⲗ ⲉ
ⲁⲅⲅⲉ
ⲉⲧⲟⲩⲁⲁⲃ
ⲥⲭⲁ ⲓ ⲩ ⲟⲉⲛ ⲇ ⲉⲕ
ⲩ ⲩⲛⲥⲙ ⲩ ⲉ
ⲏ ⲛ ⲛ ⲛⲓⲟ ⲉ ⲟ
ⲛⲟⲕⲧⲟ ⲧⲁⲗⲉⲡⲱⲣⲟⲩ
ⲓⲁⲥⲙⲟⲓ ⲉ ⲓⲗⲗⲁⲩ ⲧⲏⲣ
ⲛⲟⲩⲍⲉⲉⲥⲣ ⲧⲁⲩⲛⲁ ⲙⲛ
ⲣⲉⲩⲱⲡⲥⲟⲣ ⲓⲁⲕⲱⲛⲟⲟ
ⲉ ⲍⲣⲁⲓ ⲍⲙⲡⲉⲧⲉⲃⲱⲧ
ⲥⲟⲟⲩⲍⲁⲍⲟⲩ ⲛⲑⲟⲟⲧⲏⲏⲥⲙ

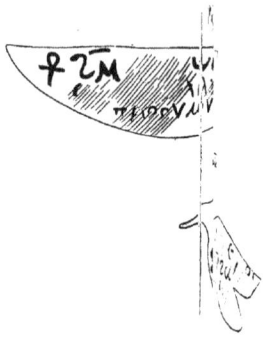

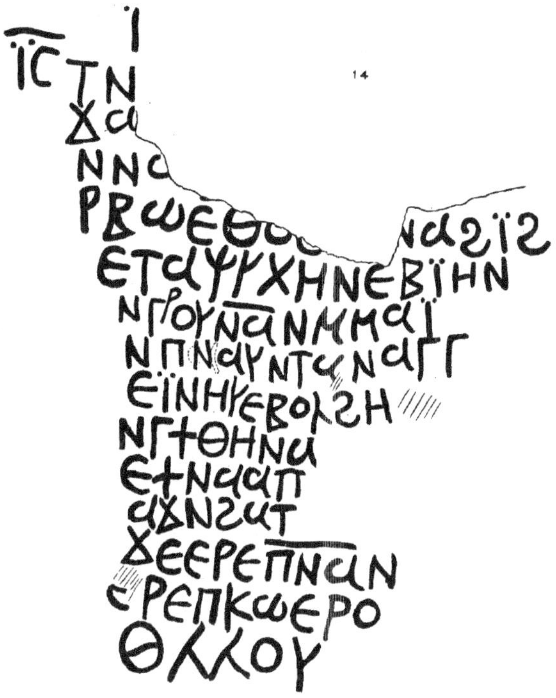

Ṭ‾Ι
Ṭ‾Ϲ ΤΝ
Χα
ΝΝϹ
ΡΒωΕΘΘ⊙⊙ⲱ ⲛⲁⲍⲓⲥ
ΕΤαΨΥΧΗΝΕΒⲓ̈ΗΝ
ΝⲄΟΥⲡⲁ‾ΝΜΜαⲓ
ΝⲠⲚαΥΝΤⲩ‾ΝαΓΓ
Εⲓ̈ΗΗⲩΕΒΟλϹΗ
ΝⲄ†ΘΗΝα
ΕⲧΝααⲡ
αⲇ‾ΝϹⲱⲧ
ΧΕΕΡΕⲠⲛⲁ‾Ν
ⲥⲢΕⲠΚωΕΡΟ
ΘλλΟΥ

Ο Μ⊙Νϲ
Μⲓ ⲁⳟⲩⲧⲓΕΝⲧⲁⲱⲡⲢα
ⲇⲉ ⲁⲅⲓⲏ†ⲧⲓⲁⲟⲩ
ⲅΟΝΝαⲚⲧⲁϹΟⲢϤΕⲧ6

ΤΑΝΤ..

ΕΙΣ Π ΝΟΥΤΕ
ΙΣΧΣ

ΕΥΛΕ

ΝΧΣΠΧΟΕΙΣΠΝΟΥΤΕ
Ν....ΑΡΕ....ΡΩΜΕΗ
ΠΕΝΤΑ........ΝΤ

ΙΕ

ΑΠΑΣ....ΒΙΝΟΕ
Τ
ΙΙΣΧΣ   ΠΑΡΧΥΜΑΝΤΡΙΤΗΣ
ΧΟΕΙΣΠΝΟΥΤΕ
ΠΑΝΤΟΗΡΑΤΟΡΕΝΑΡΟΕΙΣ
ΗΡΩΜΕΜΠΕΝΗΤ
....Ε

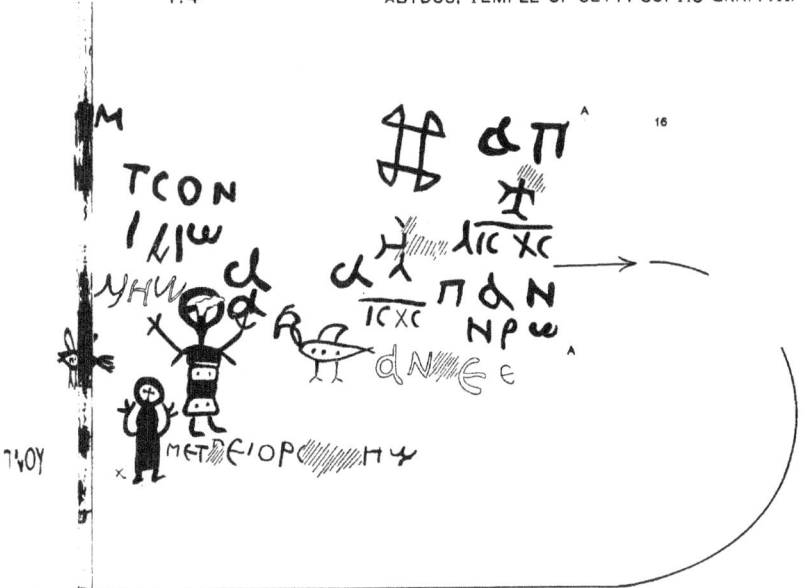

F.H.
M.A.M.

ϩⲱ
ⲇ ⲣⲧⲉ
ϭⲟⲟⲛⲉⲧⲛⲏⲕⲉⲃⲟⲓ   17

ⲁⲡⲁⲥⲁⲣⲓⲛⲟⲥⲉⲧⲟⲩⲁ   18

ⲁⲡⲟⲩⲁⲛⲛ
ⲧⲟⲕⲣⲁⲧⲣⲣ

ⲓ ⲁ ⲧⲣ ⲕ ⲟⲩⲓ   20
ⲩⲏⲁ   ⲟⲉⲓⲥ
ⲛ ⲓⲛⲟⲩⲧⲉ
ⲉⲕ   ⲛⲟⲩ
ⲣⲟ   ⲧⲉ
ⲓⲱ
ⲏⲁⲉ

ⲁⲡⲁ ⲙⲱⲩ ⲥⲏⲥ   ⲁⲡⲁⲱ   19
ⲁ ⲙ ⲁ ⲥ ⲟ ⲩ ⲓ ⲁ ⲛ ⲛ ⲁ

ⲧⲥⲟⲫⲓⲁ   21

ⲙ ⲁ ⲣ ⲓ ⲍ ⲁ ⲙ

☧ ⲁ ⲛ ⲟ ⲕ ⲁ ⲛ ⲁⲩ
ⲙ ⲓ ⲕ Ξ Δ ϩ ⲑ   Ξ ⲑ   22
Ξ ⲗ ⲭ ⲁ ⲁ ⲧ ⲣ ⲉ ⲙ
ⲛ ⲁ ⲉ ⲩ ⲥ ⲟ ⲟ   ⲁ ⲣ ⲙ   ⲁⲩ
ⲉ ⲓ ⲉ ⲣ ⲏ ⲭ ⲏ ⲧ ⲉ ⲡ ⲙ ⲟ ⲟ ⲩ ⲉ ⲓ ⲉ ϩ
ⲑ   ⲡ ⲩ ⲟ ⲩ ⲙ ϩ ⲟ ⲩ ⲛ ⲛ
ⲟⲟⲩ ⲍ   ⲟ   ⲁ ⲛ ⲟ

ⲟ ⲩ ⲁ ⲁ ⲃ ⲁ ⲟ ⲙ

23

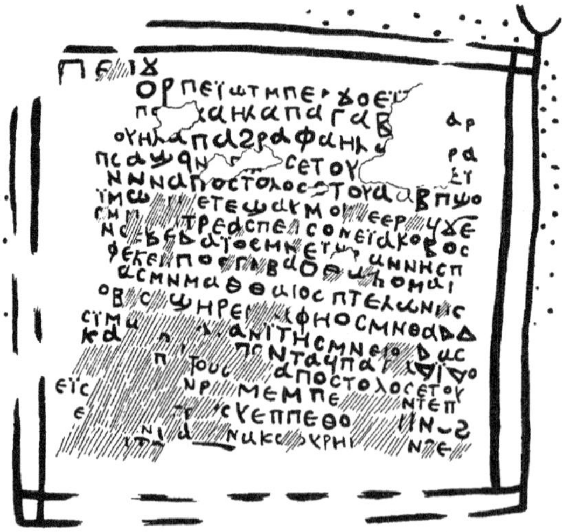

24

25

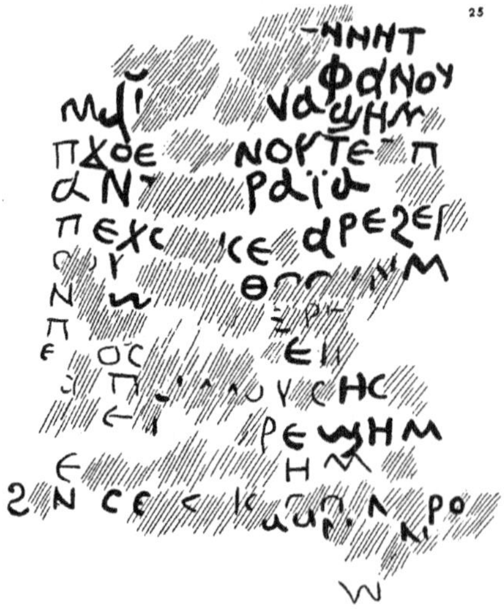

ΜΕ ΚΟΥⲰ ΗΜΜ ΠΕΡΤΗС
ⲀΝⲠ ΤΡⲀ ΚΕΜΠ ΕΡΤΗС
ⲚⲠⲞ ΕΚΟΥⲰ ΗΜ ΤΕССⲰΝ
Γ... ΓΙⲀΤΕСΜⲀ ⲀⲨ
... ΤΟΥⲰ ΗΜΤΕССⲰΝΕ
... ΤⲰΡΕⲮ ΗΜΤ ΕΥⲰΝΕ
... ΟΥΤΕⲨΜⲀⲀⲨ
ⲀⲖΟⲨⲖΕⲮΗ
ⲀΤΕСΜⲨΜ
Π... СΠ ΝΟΥΤΕ
ΠⲠⲞ ΚΡⲀΤⲰΡΕ
ΕΚⲞ СⲀΝΡΜ
ΠΕС ΤΗΡΟⲨΝΚΟⲨΪ
Ⲩ... Θ2Ι2ΟⲨΝⲀⲨⲰ
Ⲱ... ΙСΝⲀ ΝⲀⲨ
ΤⲨ ΜΕΚⲀⲖΟⲨ

M.A.M.

27

ΗΜ
ⲠⲰⲢⲨ
ⲚⲠ
ⲀⲬⲞⲈⲒⲤ
ⲈⲒⲤⲠⲀⲂⲞⲀ
ⲤⲠⲀⲰⲢ
ⲈⲨⲢⲈ
ⲢⲈⲎⲘⲈⲘⲘ
ⲢⲞⲤⲒⲤⲈⲰⲒ
ⲦⲈⲄⲒⲘⲒⲚⲞⲤ
ⲦⲒⲠⲀⲤ
ⲨⲈⲚⲠⲚⲦⲀⲄⲀⲚⲈⲂⲞ
ⲚⲀⲦⲈⲔⲘⲈⲚⲦⲈⲢⲰ
ⲦⲘⲒⲞⲒⲈⲂⲞⲀ

28

ⲠⲀⲈⲒⲤⲠⲚⲞⲨⲦⲈⲠⲀⲚⲦ
ⲦⲈⲘⲚⲀⲄⲄⲈⲀⲞⲤ
ⲀⲢⲈⲒⲄⲄⲈⲀⲞⲤ
Ⲉ ⲔⲀ̇ⲞⲤ
ⲈⲨⲔⲈⲦⲞⲨⲀⲀ
ⲔⲀⲤⲘⲞⲨⲈⲢⲞⲚ
ⲞⲒⲞⲦⲠⲀⲤⲞⲨⲰ
ⲀⲒⲀⲨ ⲦⲰⲒ
ⲒⲀ ⲦⲀⲤⲤ

29

ⲔⲀⲤⲦⲀ

30

ⲢⲈⲆⲰⲢⲀⲰⲎⲀ
ⲀⲞⲨⲆⲞⲂⲠⲀⲂⲞⲚⲰⲎⲘ
ⲘⲈⲢⲒⲦⲠⲬⲞⲈⲒⲤ
ⲚⲞⲨⲦⲈⲔⲀⲦⲚⲀⲨ
ⲨⲚ ⲦⲈⲤⲠⲀⲦⲰ

ΠⲈϢⲨⲎⲘ
ΠⲬΟⲈⲒⲤΠ ΝΟⲨⲦⲈΠΠ
ⲦⲰⲔⲀ ⲨⲢ ΟⲨⲎⲢ
ⲦΠⲈ ΠⲈ ⲎⲔⲀ ⲌΟⲨⲚ
ⲨⲢⲬⲎⲈⲢⲞⲨⲀⲀΒ ⲀⲦ
ΠⲈⲎⲌⲘⲌⲀⲖⲈ ⲉ
ⲘⲀⲈⲚⲈ ⲘⲘⲀ
ⲄⲀⲐⲰ Ν ΟΠⲦⲀⲌ
Ⲭⲱ ⲰⲤⲚⲚⲈ
ⲌⲎⲢ ⲌⲀⲢⲈⲌⲀΠ
ⲈⲬⲚⲤ Ⲕ ⲦⲰ

M.A.M.

ΒΕΕ ΕϤΕΗΡΥϹ ΒΟϤ ΤωαϤ Υ Ϲ Γ
ΤΟΓΗΡΤϤΗΗϤ
ϤΗΜΤ

ΠΙΤΕΡΙ ΛΙϹΤΑΡΟ Μ
Ρ ϤϤ
ΜΜΛΙΕΤΙΓΙΗΜΙΙϤΛ
Ε ΝΕϹωΦΗ
ΙΕΝ

ΤΑΧΗΠΙΝΤΕΜ ϤΗΝΤϤ ΙΦ   34
ΤΚ ΑϹϹΟΝΕΠ
Η   ΠΕ
ΧΟΕΙϹ ΜΟ ΤΕ

ΠΕϢΗΙΜ   35
ϤΙΠΕ ΙΦΥ ΜΠΙ ΑΓΕΟϹ
ΤΟϹ   ΙΠΙΒΙϹΙΛΙΛ

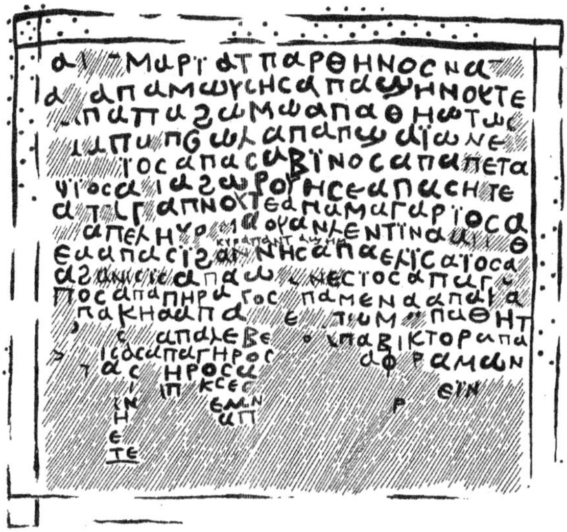

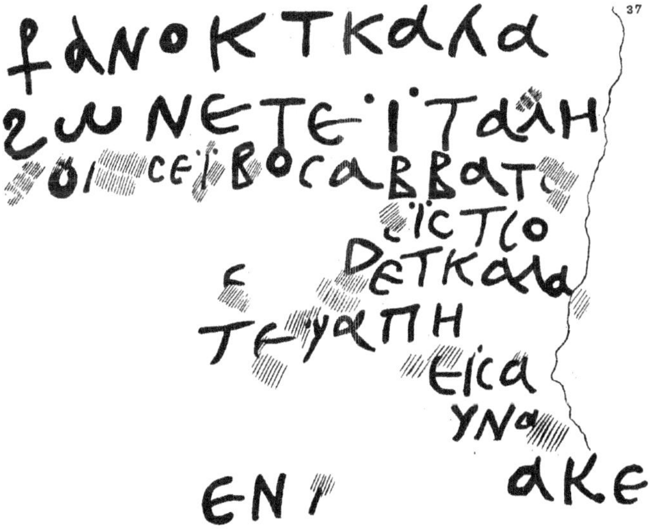

αα ε

ϊ ...υτε ... ληπορος 38

ετμεζνψονε

ιληιεζιαψαζομ

ενιιςαϊντεμτον

ζνιαϊντκοιιαυκωβ

δοιικαζ ... ζ

τεςλ

ζμπουωςϣμ

πνουτεμννεςληλ

ιινετουααβν

μο ειλ

νλολμε

κεμμε

ρηερεπεν

νς
κερ
νμη
ρομ
ρηυ
λυκ
μπς
λον
νω

ca

ιωλννλ 39
τωερε

κυρλ
νταψημ

ζιι ποιυ ει ν νν 42
ψληλννετ
ιιζουνιι ιι
λ ντμμεςον

πςωτηρ ρος 41
ιςυιυ ιςεν
τςψνος ϣηνικεαςα

πχοε πνο την
πιιμητιιψ ιιγεωπ ιο
πιςον

38

ⲢⲦⲈⲢⲈⲦⲦⲈⲚ
ⲌⲚⲀⲚⲦⲒ
ⲚⲤⲨⲘⲚⲚⲤⲰⲤⲀ
ⲔⲈⲢⲘⲠⲈⲚⲤⲞⲨⲒⲐ
ⲚⲘⲎⲱⲢⲎⲚⲤⲚⲦⲈⲚ
ⲢⲞⲘⲠⲈⲚⲤⲀⲚⲈⲨ
ⲢⲎⲨⲒⲚⲢⲘⲦⲈ
ⲀⲨⲔⲀⲦⲒ
ⲘⲠⲤⲀⲂⲀⲦⲞⲚ
ⲀⲞⲚⲀⲠⲂ
 Ⲛⲱ

ⲤⲀⲎⲚⲈ 43

Ⲓⲅ ⲒⲞⲒ ⲚⲚ 42
ⲦⲨ

ⲠⲈ ⲎⲤⲒⲤⲦⲂⲈⲨⲤ
ⲦⲒⲔⲨⲘⲞⲨ
Ⲙ Ⲣ ⲚⲨⲞⲦⲎⲢ Ⲛ ⲀⲎ Ⲉ
ⲚⲒ ⲚⲀⲚⲀⲘⲀⲔⲀⲠ ⲠⲀⲢⲦ
ⲠⲚⲞⲨⲦ Ⲉ
ⲚⲞⲨⲈⲦ

ϥⲧⲉⲛⲯⲡϩⲙⲟⲧⲛⲧⲟⲟⲧⲕⲡϫⲟⲉⲓⲥ ..
ϥⲙⲛⲟⲩⲧⲉⲡⲁⲛⲧⲱⲕⲣⲁⲧⲱⲣ
ϫⲉⲁⲕⲯⲛ̇ϩⲛ̇ⲧⲕ̇ⲁⲥⲧⲉⲛⲙⲛⲧϩⲏⲕⲉ
ⲕⲩⲛ̇ϩ̇ⲛ̇ⲧⲕⲟⲛϩⲁⲡⲉⲕⲡⲗⲁⲥⲙⲛ
ⲛⲧⲁⲕⲧⲁⲙⲓⲟ̇ϥⲁⲕⲟⲩⲱⲛϩ̇ⲧⲉⲕ
ϭⲟⲙⲉⲃⲟⲗ̇ϩ̇ⲛⲙⲉⲗⲁⲟⲥⲁⲕⲱⲙ
ⲉⲣⲟ̇ⲩⲛⲛⲥⲁⲧⲧⲟⲩⲕⲁⲓ̈ⲟ̇ⲥⲁⲕⲛ
ⲡⲙⲟⲟⲩ ⲙⲁⲛⲉⲃⲟⲩϭⲁϩⲁⲙⲉⲛⲥⲟⲩ
ϫⲟⲩⲧⲏⲗⲙⲉⲥⲟⲩⲣⲏⲙⲡⲉϩⲟⲟⲩ
ⲛⲁⲅⲁⲙⲯⲩⲥⲏⲥⲧⲉⲥⲙⲟⲩⲉⲣⲟⲕⲡⲉⲓ
ⲛⲧⲁ̇ϥⲉⲓ̈ⲥⲙⲟⲩⲉⲣⲟⲕⲡⲩⲏⲣⲉⲧⲥⲙⲟⲩ
ⲉⲓⲟⲓ ⲧⲥⲡⲓ̈ⲁⲉⲧⲟⲩⲁⲁⲃⲧⲉⲗⲉⲭⲁ
ⲣⲓ̇ⲟⲧ ⲕⲧⲱⲙⲟⲩϫⲁⲁⲕⲧⲑⲉⲛⲁⲛ
ⲕⲧⲉⲣⲟⲙⲡⲉⲧⲁⲩⲉⲧϩⲙⲩⲉⲧ
ⲉⲑⲛⲁⲛⲟⲛⲏⲧⲁ̇ⲭ̇ⲱⲕⲉ
ⲙⲁⲓ ⲓⲟⲥ̇ⲙⲓ̇ⲛⲉⲛⲁϩⲉ
ϩⲛⲙⲕⲟϩϩ ⲁ
ⲯⲁϩⲁⲛ̇ⲛⲉ
ⲯⲁ̇ⲧ·

45

ⲧⲥ̇ ⲁⲧⲙⲁ
ⲭⲟⲛ̇ⲫⲓⲥ̇ⲯⲙⲉⲥ
ⲁⲛⲟ̇ⲕⲙⲁⲣⲓⲁ̇
ⲁⲣⲓ̇ⲙⲁ̇ⲕⲁ
_ⲓ̈ⲛ̇

ЄCI   COYCⲀNNⲀ [48]

ⲀⲡⲀ NⲨⲬⲒ NⲒЄⲀⲢⲎⲦⲡЄⲚЄⲰⲦ

ⲡⲀCЄⲡⲢⲞNЄⲦⲀⲘⲞⲦⲀⲢCЄNЄ
ⲀⲡⲀⲨЄNЄⲦⲞⲘ
    Ⴆ ⲡCⲞЄⲨⲘⲀC   ⲀⲡЄⲒ
ⲔⲦⲢⲀⲀⲡⲀ NCCⲀ
ⲡⲀⲡⲀⲨⲒ —

ⲦCⲞⲨCⲀNNⲞ

ⲦCⲀ NЄ   ⲡNⲞⲨⲦЄЄⲔЄC /////ⲢⲞⲨ [49]
ⲘⲎC   ⲀⲒⲰⲢⲀ NⲎCⲦЄⲨϢЄⲢЄ
    ⲦⲂЄⲢЄ
ⲞⲦⲀⲨ

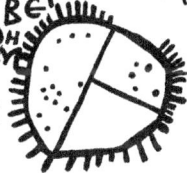

ⲀⲘⲀⲐЄⲢC
ⲂЄ·ⲔЄ

47

.

† ⲡⲗⲟⲅⲟⲥ ⲛⲛⲏⲣⲡ ⲧⲁⲛⲧⲁⲁⲩ ⲡⲕⲁⲡⲣⲱⲥⲟⲡ?
ⲡⲉϥⲁⲛ ⲡϣⲟⲥ ⲏⲣⲡ ⲓⲃ

ⲡⲇⲓⲟⲩⲣⲉ ⲁⲛⲇⲣⲁⲥ ⲑⲉⲩⲇⲱⲥⲉ ⲡⲁⲭⲱⲙ	ⲗ
ⲫⲓⲃⲁⲙⲱⲛ ⲙⲏⲛⲁ ⲭⲁⲣⲓϥ	
ⲕⲟⲥⲙⲁ ⲡⲉⲃⲙⲏ ⲡⲁⲩⲗⲉ ⲕⲟⲗⲫ	ⲗ
ⲥⲉⲩⲏⲣⲟⲥ ⲓⲱⲁⲛⲛⲏⲥ ⲡⲁϫⲱⲙ ⲡⲁⲟⲩⲁ	ⲁ
ⲫⲓⲃⲁⲙⲱⲛ ⲁⲛⲧⲱⲛⲉ ⲓⲥⲁⲕ ⲙⲁⲕⲁⲣⲉ	ⲗ
ⲥⲧⲉⲫⲛⲉ ⲑⲱⲙⲁⲥ ϯ ⲥⲧⲉⲫⲛⲉ ϯ ⲡⲓⲧⲟⲩ	
ϯ ϯ ⲕⲟⲙⲟⲥ ϯ ⲃⲱϭ ϯ ⲡⲁⲗⲟⲧⲉ ⲙⲏⲛⲁ	ⲟ
ⲡⲓⲛⲥⲉ ⲁⲡⲁ ⲕⲓⲣⲉ	
ⲑⲉⲱⲁⲣⲉ ⲕⲩⲛⲧⲓⲛⲉ ⲕⲩⲛⲧⲓⲛⲉ ⲁⲭⲱⲣⲉ	ⲗ
ⲑⲉⲱⲁⲣⲉ ⲁⲛⲑⲁⲛⲁⲥ ⲧⲉⲕⲱⲧ ⲡϣⲟⲉⲓϣ	ⲗ

ⲟⲩⲥⲟⲩⲙⲁⲭⲟⲥ	ⲗ
ⲓⲱⲁⲛⲛⲏⲥ ⲉⲣⲏⲙⲓⲁⲥ ⲭⲁⲏⲗ ⲧⲁⲣⲓⲏϥ	ⲗ
ⲁⲃⲣⲁϫⲁⲙ ⲁⲛⲧⲱⲛⲉ	ⲗ
ⲙⲁⲣⲕⲟⲥ ⲕⲟⲗⲫ ⲉⲗⲗⲱ ⲙⲁⲣⲕⲟⲥ	ⲗ
ⲙⲏⲛⲁ ⲯⲁⲧⲉ ⲁⲡⲁ ⲡⲥⲉⲛⲟⲩ	ⲗ
ⲙⲱⲥⲏⲥ ⲓⲱⲁⲛⲛⲏⲥ ⲓⲁⲕⲱⲃ ⲡϣⲟⲓ	
ⲡⲉⲃⲱϣ ⲡⲉⲥⲟⲟⲩ ⲡⲉⲃⲱϣ ⲃⲉⲗⲙⲁⲛ	ⲗ
ⲡⲉⲧⲣⲉ ⲕⲁⲗⲕⲉ ⲁⲣⲟⲟⲩ ⲓⲱⲁⲛⲛⲉ ϯ ⲡⲉⲧⲣⲉ ⲕⲁⲗⲕⲉ	ⲗ
ⲡⲁϫⲱⲙ ⲕⲁⲣⲓⲛⲓⲭ	
ϣⲉⲛⲟⲩ ⲡⲥⲁⲃⲁⲩⲛⲉ	ⲗ

ⲙⲱⲥⲏⲥ ⲡϣⲟⲉⲓϣ ϣⲟⲙⲛⲧ ⲛⲉⲃⲱϣ ⲟⲩⲣⲱⲙⲉ ϣⲉⲕⲟⲩⲧⲉ ϩⲁⲡϣⲓⲧⲟⲩ	ⲇ ⲁ ⲁ
ⲭⲱⲱⲣⲉ ⲕⲱⲥⲛⲧⲏ ⲇⲁⲛⲓⲏⲗ ⲱ ? ?	ⲗ
ⲑⲉⲱⲇⲁⲣⲉ ⲙⲱⲥⲏⲥ ⲡⲁⲙⲫⲓⲗⲗⲟⲥ	
ⲛϣⲓ ⲛⲇⲓⲟⲩⲧⲕ	
ⲁⲛⲑⲁⲛⲁⲥⲉ ⲥⲉⲩⲏⲣⲟⲥ ⲁⲕⲉⲛⲏ ⲥⲉⲩⲏⲣⲟⲥ	ⲗ
ⲡⲁⲧⲣⲉⲙⲟⲩⲧ ⲕⲏⲥⲉ	ⲃ
ⲗⲟⲕⲁⲥ ⲙⲁⲣⲕⲟⲥ	
ⲕⲟⲗⲫ ⲕⲏⲥⲉ ⲅⲉⲱⲣⲅⲉ ⲇⲁⲛⲓⲗ	
ⲁⲛⲟⲩⲡ ⲟⲛⲟⲩⲫⲣⲉ ⲫⲓⲃⲁⲙⲟⲛ ⲇⲁⲛⲓⲏⲗ	ⲗ
ⲉⲗⲉⲙⲁⲓⲟⲥ ⲗⲉⲱⲛⲧⲓⲟⲥ ⲡⲉⲛⲩ ϯ ⲉⲗⲉⲙⲁ?	

---

† ⲕⲟⲥⲙⲁ ⲅⲁⲉ..ⲱⲣⲉϩ ⲛϣⲓ ⲛⲧⲕⲟⲩⲛⲛⲉ	}
ⲁⲡⲁ ⲕⲓⲣⲉ ⲙⲱⲥⲏⲥ ϯ ⲙⲏⲛⲁ ⲡⲉⲧⲣⲱⲛⲉ ϯ ⲓⲱⲥⲏⲫ ⲕⲁⲗⲉ	ⲗ
ⲡⲁⲛⲧⲓⲛⲉ	ⲋ
ⲧⲓⲙⲓⲁⲛⲟⲥ ⲡⲉⲕⲱⲧ ⲗⲁⲕⲉⲕ ϥⲧⲟⲟⲩ ⲛⲃⲱⲃ	ⲗ ⲗ
ⲡϣⲟⲓ ⲯⲁⲭⲱ	ⲗ
ⲑⲱⲙⲁⲥ ⲑⲉⲱⲁⲣⲉ ϯ ⲡⲁⲟⲩ	ⲗ
ⲡϣⲟⲓ ⲑⲉⲱⲁⲣⲉ	ⲗ
ⲟⲛⲟⲩⲫⲣⲉ ⲓⲁⲕⲱⲃ	ⲗ
ⲥⲉⲏϥ ⲙⲁⲣⲑⲁ ⲕⲁⲙⲉⲗ ⲕⲁⲗⲓⲛⲓⲕⲟⲥ ⲡⲉϣⲁⲧⲉ ⲙⲉⲣⲕⲱ ⲡ.ϩⲁⲣⲓⲟⲩ.ⲡⲉ..ⲉ ⲡⲉⲥⲛⲧⲉ ⲑⲉⲱⲁⲣⲉ	ⲗ ⲗ ⲃ
ⲡⲉⲧⲣⲉ ⲁⲡⲁ ⲕⲓⲣⲉ ⲡⲉⲧⲣⲉ ? ?	?

Ostracon.

Two Steles.

ⲡⲣⲟⲫⲏⲧ
ⲛⲁⲡⲟⲥⲧⲟⲗⲟⲥ
ⲙⲙⲁⲣⲧⲩⲣⲟⲥ
ⲛⲉⲧⲟⲩⲁⲁⲃ ⲧⲏ
ⲣⲟⲩ ⲁⲣⲓ ⲡⲙⲉ
ⲉⲩⲉ ⲛⲡⲁⲥⲟⲛ
ⲡⲁⲩⲗⲉ ⲇⲉⲙⲧⲟⲛ
ⲙⲙⲟⲩ ⲛⲥⲟⲩⲭⲟⲩ
ⲧⲯⲓⲥ ⲙⲡⲁⲩⲱⲛⲉ
ϩⲛⲟⲩⲉⲓⲣⲏⲛⲏ ϩⲁ
ⲙⲏⲛ ϯ ⲓ ⲓⲛⲇ

Ⲏ ⲁⲅⲓⲁ ⲧⲣⲓⲁⲥ ⲉϥⲕⲏ ⲉϩⲣⲁⲓ
ⲙⲡⲉⲓⲙⲁ ⲛϭⲓ ⲡⲉⲥⲕⲏⲛⲟⲙⲁ
ⲙⲡⲁⲡⲉⲓⲣⲡⲙⲉⲉⲩⲉ. ⲉⲧⲛⲁⲛⲟⲩϥ
ⲡⲙⲁⲕⲁⲣⲓⲟⲥ ⲁⲡⲁ ⲑⲉⲟⲇⲱⲣⲟⲥ ⲡⲱⲛ
ⲣⲉ ⲙⲡⲙⲁⲕⲁⲣⲓⲟⲥ ⲙⲱⲩⲥⲏⲥ ⲡⲉⲡⲣⲉⲥ
ⲃⲩⲧⲉⲣⲟⲥ ⲡⲣⲙⲧⲡⲟⲗⲩⲃⲓⲁⲛⲏ ⲛⲧⲁϥ
ⲙⲧⲟⲛ ⲇⲉ ⲙⲙⲟϥ ⲫⲁⲙⲉⲛⲱⲑ ⲙⲉ
ⲛⲟⲥ ⲃ ⲁⲡⲟ ⲇⲓⲟⲕⲗⲩⲧⲓⲁⲛⲟⲩ ⲭⲛⲉ
ⲉⲣⲉⲡⲛⲟⲩⲧⲉ ϯⲙⲧⲟⲛ ⲛⲧⲉϥⲯⲩⲭⲏ
ⲛⲉⲩⲛⲟⲭⲩ ⲉⲕⲟⲩⲛϥ ⲛⲁⲃⲣⲁϩⲁⲙ
ⲙⲛⲓⲥⲁⲕ ⲙⲛⲓⲁⲕⲱⲃ ⲛⲉϥⲃⲁⲗ
ⲛⲙⲡϣⲁ ⲛⲥⲱⲧⲙ ⲉⲧⲟⲥⲙⲏ
ⲉⲧⲙⲉϩ ⲛⲛⲁ ϩⲓⲙⲧⲩⲉⲗⲗⲉ
ϩⲧⲏϥ ⲇⲉⲁⲙⲏⲉⲓⲧⲛ ⲛⲉⲧⲥⲙⲁ
ⲙⲁⲁⲧ ⲛⲧⲉ ⲡⲁⲉⲓⲱⲧ ⲛⲧⲉⲧⲛ
ⲕⲗⲏⲣⲟⲛⲟⲙⲉⲓ ⲛⲧⲙⲓⲛⲧⲉⲣⲟ ⲛⲧⲁⲩ
ⲥⲃⲧⲱⲧⲉ ⲛⲏⲧⲛ ϫⲓⲛⲧⲕⲁⲧⲁⲃⲟⲗⲏ
ⲙⲡⲕⲟⲥⲙⲟⲥ ⲙⲟ ⲡⲉⲭⲥ ⲁⲙⲏⲛ
ⲉϥⲉϣⲱⲡⲉ

CPSIA information can be obtained at www.ICGtesting.com
Printed in the USA
BVOW06s1049310816

460720BV00019B/167/P

9 781332 620173